TO DO . . .
DOING . . .
DONE!

A Creative Approach to Managing
Projects and Effectively Finishing
What Matters Most

G. LYNNE SNEAD AND JOYCE WYCOFF

A FIRESIDE BOOK
Published by Simon & Schuster

FIRESIDE
Rockefeller Center
1230 Avenue of the Americas
New York, NY 10020

FIRESIDE and colophon are registered trademarks
of Simon & Schuster Inc.

Designed by Irving Perkins Associates, Inc.

Manufactured in the United States of America

20 19 18 17 16 15 14 13 12 11

Library of Congress Cataloging-in-Publication Data
is available.

ISBN 0-684-81887-6

ACKNOWLEDGMENTS

From Lynne Snead:

I believe we are what we think.

Small successes build our confidence and self-esteem and lead to larger successes.

Many of those successes come from getting the important things done in our lives, the things we value most. Peter Drucker said efficiency is doing things right, effectiveness is doing the right things. This book is about knowing what is important to us and making the right things happen the right way. But it's really about the inner peace and well-being that come from those successful results.

I would like to thank the people who helped me know and realize that the only limitations in my life were in my own thinking and by changing my thinking I could change my reality. Our dreams are there as seeds to garden with love and care. They could not be there if they could not come true.

This book is a result of support from many people who helped me create reality out of a dream. This long list includes Hyrum Smith, Dick Winwood, Leigh Stevens, Jana Buchanan, and Don Atkinson. Special thanks to my family, who believed in my work and helped me create the space and time in which to do it. I am very grateful for their support.

Brenda Peterson said, "The soul of genius is in the revision." My deep thanks to one of the best editors, and best friends, I have ever had, Marna McComb, without whose editing patience and overall support this book would have never become a reality.

Special thanks to my life teachers and mentors for helping

me know who I am and what I could be—my parents and Sue and Tom Feltz. This would not be if it weren't for you.

Thanks to James Young and Deborah Larson, for their significant contributions, and to the entire team of twenty-five PFR consultants who are on the road tirelessly teaching the Planning For Results seminar to hundreds of people every month. You are the continuous improvement process by which we have learned, tested, and improved this system.

My sincere thanks to Joyce. This book has been a dream of mine for a long time, but writing a book is unquestionably one of the most challenging projects I have ever undertaken. Joyce paved the way through her experience, her talent and creativity, her commitment and dedication, and her friendship. This project became a reality with quality that never would have been possible without her.

From Joyce Wycoff:

Sometimes projects are interesting, sometimes they're fun and sometimes they're rewarding. Occasionally a project comes along that's all three. Writing this book with Lynne definitely falls into that category. I'm grateful to Lynne for sharing this project, which is based on her life passion. It has been enlightening, fulfilling, and a great deal of fun.

From Lynne and Joyce:

Our undying gratitude to the two people who championed this project from the very beginning and whose dedication helped make it a reality: Dawn Daniels, a wonderful editor, and Denise Stinson, a truly remarkable agent. Thank you both for your hard work and friendship.

CONTENTS

Project Managers—Linchpins of the New Organization

How does a major project get to be a year late?
One day at a time.

—Tom Peters
quoting a software pioneer
in *The Pursuit of Wow!*

In the work world of the 1990s, projects have become a way of life, and the ability to manage projects is a critical skill. People who can take a project from idea to completion are increasingly in demand, and people who don't have those skills will be left behind in a world that continues to downsize, rightsize, and just plain lay off process managers.

Project management is "the wave of the future," says an in-house newsletter from the technology and training group at General Motors. William Dauphinais, a partner at Price Waterhouse, also believes that project management is an increasingly important skill. In an interview with *Fortune* magazine, July 10, 1995, he stated, "Project management is going to be huge in the next decade. The project manager is the linchpin in the horizontal-vertical organizations we're creating."

Until recently, most people went to work every day knowing that they would do pretty much the same thing they had done the day before. People often worked for the same employer for the bulk of their careers, progressing from an entry-level job to a supervisory or management position within the same department or plant. They were recognized and promoted based on their expertise in the *processes* of their department or function—processes that stayed basically the same year after year.

PROCESS MANAGEMENT SKILLS ARE NO LONGER ENOUGH

Those days are gone. We are now in a period of change—rapid change. New technologies, global markets, and aggressive competition have changed all the rules. Companies are running faster and faster just to survive. Continuous improvement is no longer enough; quantum leaps are mandatory. This pressure-cooker environment creates a constant pressure to do more with less and has completely changed the nature of work for most people. Long-term job security is an obsolete concept, frequent career changes are the norm, and few employees can survive on their day-to-day process abilities alone.

Project: a nonroutine series of tasks directed toward a goal

Almost every employee, regardless of job title, spends more and more time focused on projects. Defined as a complex of nonroutine tasks directed toward meeting a specific goal, projects are now commonplace at all levels of every organization. Secretaries may be involved in implementing a new administrative system, purchasing word processing equipment, or planning a corporate event. Front-line manufacturing personnel may serve on a team that designs a product improvement requested by a customer, or they may work on a project to reengineer the entire plant. Supervisors may be responsible for writing a new policy or managing a cost-cutting initiative. In short, everyone is now required to be a project completion expert.

Success depends on the ability to effectively complete projects.

In our increasingly demanding world, the people who succeed will be the ones who can initiate, manage, and complete challenging projects. They will be the ones who know how to create a vision that engages everyone involved in the project. They will be able to define expected results; delegate responsibility; break the project down into bite-size tasks; develop achievable schedules; communicate concisely, clearly, and rapidly; adjust quickly to changes; monitor progress; and accept nothing short of project success.

WHERE DO PEOPLE LEARN THESE NEW SKILLS?

If you ask any person in any company, "What project are you working on?" you'll generally get at least one answer, and more likely, more than one. In addition to their normal daily duties, most people in the organization will be involved in one or more nonroutine sets of tasks or projects. But who teaches these people how to effectively manage and complete their projects?

Schools don't. Even business and engineering programs seldom teach students how to complete projects effectively. And only a handful of businesses teach their employees these critical skills.

Projects are very different from processes and require unique skills. While processes are ongoing and often designed to generate or maintain revenue flow, projects are temporary resource-consuming efforts designed to achieve a specific goal. Using limited resources, with often severe time constraints and aggressive goals, projects can easily get bogged down in conflicts or internal politics, sidetracked by internal or external changes, or just lost in the daily grind.

To Do . . . Doing . . . Done! A Creative Approach to Man-

aging Projects and Effectively Finishing What Matters Most builds on the concepts of time management and then goes beyond them to provide a simple model to help you become a project completion expert.

Beyond time management to project completion

To Do . . . Doing . . . Done! is based on well-established techniques and principles which, to date, have not been readily available to the average person. Many sophisticated project completion tools were developed and refined in the 1960s as the space program became a reality. Tools such as PERT charts, Gantt charts, and critical path analyses were used by technical specialists in the military, the government, and the defense industry. These projects generally involved hundreds or thousands of people, millions of dollars' worth of resources, and months or years to complete. Most of us, however, need to manage much simpler projects and we need powerful yet easy-to-use tools that we can use to complete any project more effectively.

To Do . . . Doing . . . Done! brings project completion out of the realm of "for technical experts only" and puts its high-powered tools into the hands of the masses. It cuts through academic jargon and spells out a simple process that anyone can use to achieve his or her objectives more effectively. This book gives you everything you need to become a *project completion expert,* from a simple technique to help generate ideas more creatively to a complete set of tools for tracking tasks and schedules through completion.

Simple tools . . . high-powered results

The project and workload management concepts in this book can be used by anyone—from a corporate president launching a new product to a den mother planning a weekend camping trip; from a research scientist working on a new wonder drug to a student studying for the SATs; from the designers of the space program to the homeowner remodeling a kitchen.

HOW TO USE THIS BOOK

This book is divided into three primary sections and two appendixes to help you pick and choose the material you need most. Dive in any place that makes sense for you and your situation. Here's a brief description of the sections.

Section I: To Do—Choosing Your Projects Wisely

It's much easier to complete projects successfully if we are enthusiastic about them and if they match our personal values. This section helps you identify your values and choose projects that are consistent with your values.

Also, all projects begin with an idea. This section helps you understand how your mind works and how to enhance your personal creativity and apply it to your projects.

If these ideas are new to you, we suggest a careful reading. If they're familiar, you may just want to skim through and note the gems and Ponder Points.

Section II: Organizing Your Time and the Flood of Information

Time and information management are crucial to effective project management. If you are already effectively using a day planner and are in control of the information that flows into your office, you can skip this section. If you aren't using a day planner, however, Chapter 4 is a must.

If you could save a small forest by recycling the paper on your desk, check out Chapter 5. It's a painless way (really!) to get control of the flood of data that comes your way every day.

Section III: Doing . . . and **Done!** *Making Project Completion Easy*

Yes, you can skip immediately to Section III! This is *your* book. Make it work for you. It's fine to jump into the project management model and then go back and pick up other points from previous sections as you realize they're important and as you need them. This is not a novel, so it's just fine to know the outcome before you begin. However, there is a progression to all of this, so at some point, you'll want to skim through the first two sections to see if there's any information there that you might be missing.

BOOK FORMAT

Throughout this book, we will help you find easier and more effective ways to accomplish results. To help you learn and remember the ideas presented, we have included the following format helpers:

- **Coming Attractions.** On the first page of each chapter you'll find coming attractions in which the main chapter ideas are highlighted.
- **Frameworks and Models.** Theories and principles have been reduced to visual models that will help you thoroughly understand the material.
- **Ponder Points.** In the theoretical sections, you will find Ponder Points, which give you a chance to take a mental break and think about how the material relates to your particular situation.

WE ARE ALL PROJECT MANAGERS

If you are still wondering whether this book is for you, stop and think for a moment about the work that you do during an average day. Think not only about what you do all day long but also about the things you'd like to do but haven't gotten to yet—like adding a room to your house, improving your filing system, writing a novel, building a warehouse, getting a professional certification, or raising money for your favorite charity. It quickly becomes apparent that we are all project managers.

This book is for all of you. It is designed to help you make your hopes and dreams come true . . . a way to turn your ideas into reality.

A NOTE ABOUT THE AUTHORS

Lynne and Joyce met while both were at a shifting point in their careers. Lynne was developing a kernel of an idea about starting a project management workshop to supplement the existing Franklin Covey Co. Time Management offering. Joyce had just gotten a contract for her first book, *Mindmapping: Your Personal Guide to Exploring Creativity and Problem-Solving.*

They discovered that they shared a broad base of philosophies and values, and they began a series of collaborations, which often led to discussions about what "the project management book" would look like. In a joint venture such as this book, it's often hard to discover where one person's ideas end and another's begin but the foundation for the book is Lynne's passion for and years of experience with project and workload management. Throughout the book, Lynne relates many of her experiences and examples in the first person. Therefore, wherever you see "I" you will be hearing Lynne's stories and experiences.

Lynne and Joyce both hope you will find the following material life-enhancing.

TO DO:

CHOOSING YOUR PROJECTS WISELY

When our eyes see our hands doing the work of our hearts,
the circle of Creation is completed inside us,
the doors of our souls fly open and
love steps forth to heal everything in sight.

—MICHAEL BRIDGE

IT'S NOT JUST ABOUT WORK

Project management isn't just about being more effective at work. As a project management consultant and the author and developer of Franklin Covey's Planning for Results project and workload management seminar, I have spent much of the past seven years traveling nationally and internationally, teaching and discussing project management with thousands of individuals from hundreds of organizations.

This is what I hear from class participants time and time again: "I have my regular job, and *then* there are my projects." Translation: projects are what we do on top of our daily job requirements. I don't know of many professionals these days who work a forty-hour week. Work and work stress seem to spill over into the rest of our lives, and in doing so, they often throw our lives out of balance, increasing the stress to a frustrating and sometimes hazardous level.

It's about bringing life into balance.

Learning to effectively manage and finish the projects we begin helps bring our lives back into balance. Not only do we learn how to complete projects more effectively in less time but the simple process outlined in this book also shows us how to choose projects that match our life values. Understanding how our projects align with our life direction stimulates commitment and energy for those projects, reducing stress and making us more effective.

This book is for all of you who want practical help managing your projects more effectively. Until now, such a quest would have required a frustrating array of books and seminars filled with complicated concepts and jargon and designed for technical experts who are building space shuttles or skyscrapers. Those complex resources are definitely not geared to help those of us who just need to get the latest project done or who have an idea we'd like to turn into a reality.

This book offers not a technical approach but rather a practical and creative approach to project management—I like to think of it as project management for the masses. It's for those of us who need to manage sometimes small, sometimes large projects while at the same time balancing our workload with all the other elements of our life.

A CREATIVE APPROACH

All projects begin with an idea; therefore projects are the way we bring our ideas into reality. While I was teaching a seminar for an automobile manufacturing company, one participant was disturbed that what I was teaching was not consistent enough with their problem-solving class curriculum. His concept of projects was that they came from problems. Period. However, if we initiate projects only when a problem arises, we become locked into a reactive, crisis management mode. This person didn't seem to understand that our projects can also come from our values, from our dreams, and from chance opportunities . . . or from problems that need to be solved.

Everything begins with an idea.

Most of the project management classes I have attended and books I have read begin by clarifying and defining a project. But if a project begins with an idea, shouldn't we spend some time thinking about how we generate those ideas? Shouldn't the creative aspect of project management be just as important as the clarifying and defining?

Creativity is a key element of project management, yet most project management books and seminars never mention the word. Most focus solely on the technical aspects, with the result that creativity is lost or diminished in importance. The project management trade journals are full of articles written by academics, many of whom are out to prove to other academics how intelligent they are, and while there is occasionally a helpful tip or technique, I have never read an article in those journals specifically about the creative aspects of project management. Chapter 2 will show you the connection between creativity and successfully defining, managing, and completing a project.

IT'S ALL ABOUT INNER PEACE

Truly effective project management, however, rests on an even deeper foundation. Our dreams, goals, and ideas come from our values. Values are simply the principles and qualities we care about most. While they may be different for each of us, all individuals have values and all organizations have values. If what we are doing does not come from what we care about most in life, it is meaningless. You may complete a well-managed project, but if that project wasn't supported by your values and those of your organization, it will not lead to a sense of personal satisfaction and accomplishment.

Hyrum Smith, vice chairman and one of the founders of Franklin Quest (now Franklin Covey Co.), believes that aligning our values with the projects we manage is a critical element of inner peace. In a recent conversation he explained how he makes this connection in his time management seminars:

> The theme that permeates the entire time management seminar is the acquisition and maintenance of inner peace. That's what it's all about. I've taught lots of seminars, and often I'll start the seminar by asking, "Why did you come to this class?"
>
> The first response is almost always the same. They'll say, "I want to be more productive." Then I ask them why they want to be more productive, and they'll think about it and generally say something like "Well, I could get more stuff done." Then I ask them why they want to get more stuff done, and by the time I've asked the question four or five times, we always get to the same answer: "I'm in this class because I want to feel better."
>
> Being in control feels better than being out of control. Quite frankly, if people can learn to manage projects—from massive projects such as building an automobile down to building a boat in my basement—if people can learn to do that better, faster, more efficiently, with greater satisfaction, then that's right in line with what we're all about as a company—helping people get better control of their lives. If I can better manage my projects at work, I will, in fact, be able to spend more time with my family and I won't have all the stress marks of being out of control.

The end result of being able to efficiently and effectively complete the projects we choose to work on is an important strategy for developing inner peace and life harmony. The following chapters will help you develop that strategy.

CHAPTER 1

CREATING A PERSONAL VISION

What you must dare is to be yourself.

—DAG HAMMARSKJÖLD

The subject matter of this chapter changed my life and made this book possible.

In 1985 I was a marketing director and project manager for a computer engineering company in Utah. The word that best describes how I was feeling at that time of my life is "overwhelmed," although "out of control" also comes close. I had recently taken on these new positions and really didn't know how to get the job responsibilities under control and properly managed.

One day the president of the company announced a new training program offered by a company then called the Franklin Institute. Not wanting to hear from his often outspoken staff, the president didn't tell us what the training was, just when and where to show up. Having seen many training initiatives come and go, when I walked into the conference room and saw a day planner and training guidebook at each seat, I remember thinking, What harebrained idea are we chasing this time?

Although I didn't realize it completely at the time, by the end of the day, my life had changed forever. During the session we learned how to use a day planner to get control of our time, to track and manage all those tasks that had previously slipped through the cracks. I also learned how to develop a referencing system that kept all that old-but-still-important information at my fingertips. I remember the excitement and the sense that I might be able to get my new job responsibilities under control by using this tool.

But one part of the training day bothered me a lot. The presenter talked about building our productivity on the basis of our own personal values. He led us through an exercise to identify our values, defining them as the principles and qualities we cared most about in our lives. His point was that if our productivity was based on something other than our personal values, then even if we managed our time better and became more productive, we wouldn't be more personally satisfied.

Being more productive may not mean being more satisfied.

Philosophically that made sense to me, and I was amazed that I had never identified and prioritized my values before. The problem came when I actually had my list of values in front of me. Here were the things that I thought were most important in my life, yet when I compared my list to the life I was living, they didn't seem to have much in common.

During that one-day training session, we didn't have enough time to fully develop and clarify our values, so during the next few weeks I finished the exercise. Working a little each day, I drew up a list of nine personal values, defined and clarified what they meant to me, and developed goals that related to each value. Since then I have added values to that list, but those original nine have never changed. They defined the qualities I felt were critical in my life, such as having a warm, healthy relationship with my son (at the time, I was a single mother of a seven-year-old), continuing my growth and development mentally and spiritually, financial security, healthy relationships, health and fitness, and so forth.

The hardest part of working with these values was ranking them. I realized that while they were all vital to me, some were of higher value than others. The value that became my number one priority surprised me at the time, but I couldn't have chosen a better guidance system for how I wanted to live my life. It was "Inner peace and well-being."

Once I had my values identified and goals defined for each, I could develop the list of specific daily tasks that would lead toward those goals. These tasks were plugged in to my day planner where they became more than just tasks; they were stepping-stones toward the life I wanted to lead.

It's hard to describe what happened, but my life today, twelve years later, bears little resemblance to the life I was living then. The changes came unfailingly, sometimes slowly and sometimes rapidly, sometimes in expected ways but often from completely unexpected directions. Hyrum Smith often mentions that a plane flying from Los Angeles to Honolulu may be off course as much as 97 percent of the time! However, because the pilot knows exactly where the destination is, as soon as the plane veers slightly off course, he makes a correction. Getting to our destination does not require perfection; it simply requires a clear picture of where we're going and a willingness to change course as often as it takes to get there.

⌘ ***Ponder Point:*** *Can you think of a time in your life when you were often off course but, through frequent corrections, wound up where you wanted to be?*

One of my first changes came when I realized that my list of values was incompatible with my job situation. It took a little more than a year, but with my values list in mind, I was eventually able to find an employer who was a better fit with my life direction.

I also began to make progress on my other values, such as developing my intellectual and career growth through evening classes and reading as many books as possible, studying to become a practitioner in my church, focusing on health and physical fitness, and rearranging my schedule to have more time to spend with my son. None of this happened overnight, but gradually what I had clarified as my values steadily became my lifestyle. Now, as I look at my list of values, I can see that it has become my life, not just a wish list.

JUST SAY YES

Identifying and prioritizing our life values is the first step in developing a life purpose, a process that may be the most important work we do in our life. Purpose pulls us in the direction we want to go. Many popular reform programs are based on a philosophy of "Just say no!" Unfortunately, those programs generally are not very successful because saying no to something is not as powerful as saying yes to an objective that we are passionate about.

Purpose pulls us in the direction we want to go.

For example, a friend of mine, after several years of working as a sales manager, recently reached a crossroads. His company had gone public, which created a sizable windfall for him. While it wasn't like winning Super Lotto, it was enough money to give Kevin some options—travel, luxuries, retirement, even possibly a few harmful indulgences.

But for Kevin the decision was easy because he had a life purpose. He had spent time identifying his life values, and he was clear about his biggest dream: establishing a camp for high-risk adolescents. He knew exactly what he wanted the camp to look like and how it would be operated. When the windfall came his way, he knew with great certainty what to do with it. Without that clear vision of his life purpose, Kevin might have used the money for things that would not have brought him the joy that building a camp for kids is now bringing him.

For several years the corporate world has emphasized the importance of mission or vision statements. Well-thought-out vision statements provide a road map to guide the actions and decisions of people throughout the organization. Exciting, challenging vision statements engage the energies and enthusiasms of people, often creating incredible levels of peak performance. Just as vision statements help guide and motivate organizations, personal vision statements help individuals reach their highest level.

> ⌘ ***Ponder Point:*** *Before continuing, write a one-sentence vision statement for your life. Notice whether this is an easy or difficult exercise. The more difficult it is, the more useful you will find the following material.*

For a personal vision statement to be effective, however, it has to be based on our deepest values. A vision statement of being the richest person in the world would be counterproductive for a person whose governing value was spending time with family or becoming a concert pianist.

IDENTIFYING OUR GOVERNING VALUES

Sometimes people get concerned when we talk about values, because they think we're preaching or trying to impose our beliefs or principles on them. The following exercise is not about which values are right or wrong, good or bad. It's about understanding what's important in your life. I am passionate about nature and horses, and I love to spend time riding. For Joyce, riding horses is a pleasant diversion rather than a passion, and I'm sure there are folks who would consider riding a torture and see no value in it at all.

Values tell us *why* we do what we do.

By identifying our governing values, we begin to understand why we do what we do. Values are the underlying motivators of all of our actions. Living effectively means that everything we do is based on one or more of our values. One of my values is family, so when I hang out with my son or have a leisurely Sunday barbecue with my parents, that time is just as important as time spent working. Eventually we can look at each of our actions and ask ourselves what value is being supported by that action. We can also see gaps where our life is not supporting certain values, thus creating a life out of balance.

Jot down five things you've done in the past few days and then identify the values related to those activities. We've provided four examples to get you started.

Activity	Values
Riding my horse	Nature, solitude, inner peace
Going to a movie	Family time
Kayaking	Adventure, nature
Going to work	Financial security, contribution
_____	_____
_____	_____
_____	_____
_____	_____
_____	_____

One of the best ways to discover your values is to use a simple technique called "mindmapping." We will discuss this technique further in the next chapter, but for now, take the next five minutes and complete the mindmap template on page 28 with the principles and qualities that are most important to your life. For these few minutes, don't think about the *should*s or *ought to*s. These are *your* values, not your parents', teachers', bosses'—yours! Spend a few minutes mapping your values and we'll talk more about these values in the coming chapters. You can build on the activities and values you identified above. The following questions may help you identify even more values that are most important in your life:

What are all the qualities that make your life better?
What helps you survive, thrive, and prosper?
What would you like to have more of in your life?
What would you miss if it were eliminated from your life?
What qualities define the person you want to be?

As you're filling in the values map in Figure 1-1, put down everything that comes to mind; you can always go back later and combine, edit, or delete. This is just a first look at your values. We will explore this further in Chapter 3 when we use these values as a basis for building a foundation for personal and organizational projects.

Here's a sample list of values to help stimulate your thinking:

GOVERNING VALUES _____

Family	Productivity
Health and fitness	Honesty
Financial security	Generosity
Friends	Organization
Beauty	Fun
Inner peace	Joy
Growth	Community

Frugality	Leadership
Music	Nature
Travel	Learning
Spirituality	Career growth and development
Achievement	Freedom
Adventure	Wisdom
Love	

Once you have a mindmap of your values, you have an image of what your ideal life would be like since it would include all of the values on your mindmap. You can begin to look at your present situation and make adjustments to add

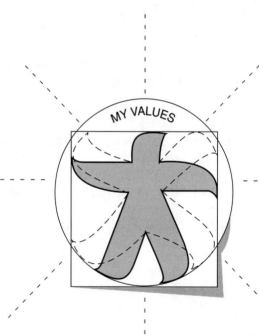

FIGURE 1-1
My Values

things that aren't present in your life or eliminate activities that are not consistent with your life values. You can use this values map as a constant reminder of what you want your life to be like. It helps you make decisions about your career, where to live, how to invest your money, who to choose as a spouse, even how much to eat or exercise.

Your values map helps you make important decisions about your life.

VALUES BALANCING

Here's a quick exercise to give you a visual clue about how well balanced your life is.

Take your top values and put them in the box at the end of each spoke of the value balance wheel (Figure 1-2). Then turn to the performance indicator form (Figure 1-3) and think about where you'd like to be with each value. For instance, if one of your values is financial security, you might consider the following objectives perfect for right now:

- Saving 10 percent of each paycheck
- Having no credit card debt
- Accumulating an investment portfolio of $10,000

Fill in your current perfect performance for each value.

HOW ARE YOU DOING?

If you're doing all of the activities that you determined would be perfect for a particular value, give yourself a 10 and put a dot on the spoke next to that value box. However, in the above example, let's assume that you haven't quite accomplished

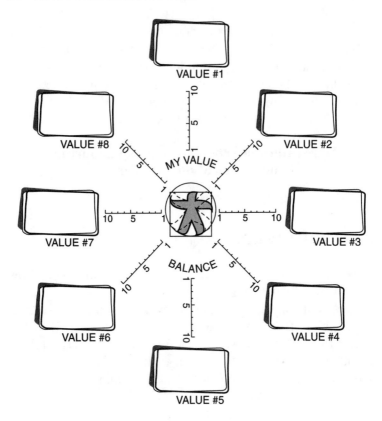

FIGURE 1-2
Values Balancing

everything that you'd like: you've missed a couple of pay periods on your savings, and you still have some balances on your credit card. In that case, you might put a dot on the 7. If you haven't saved anything for several months and you're not making progress on your credit card debt or your investment portfolio, you might give yourself a 1 or a 2. This is your evaluation of how you're doing.

Go around the wheel and rate your *current* performance on each value. Remember, this isn't some rating against a future perfect ideal; this is just how are you doing right now

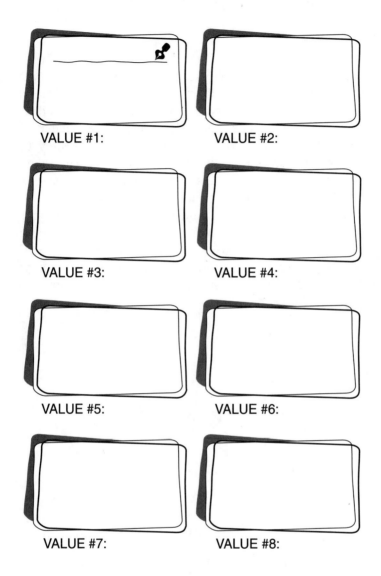

FIGURE 1-3
Performance Indicators

compared to a reasonable target for this particular value. Once you've rated yourself on each of the values, you can connect the dots and you have an image of how balanced your life is. You will probably find yourself with a somewhat lop-sided circle—relatively high numbers for some of the values and low ones for a few. This gives you an immediate take on where your life is out of balance and shows you where extra effort could help bring your life into better balance.

Knowing what you want your life to look like is an important first step to living effectively. This creates the foundation for the things we want to be able to create in our lives, for ourselves as individuals, and for organizations. To help you create the life you want, the next chapter will explore your gift of creativity.

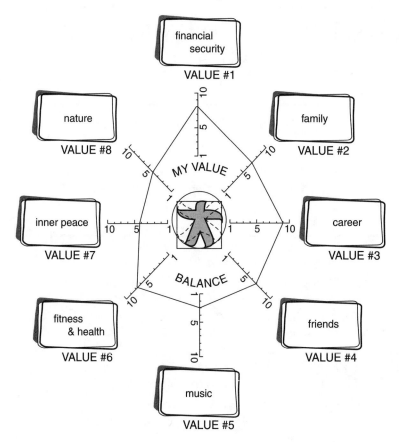

Instructions:

1. Determine current ideal performance for each value in Figure 1-3
2. Rate your current actual performance and place a dot by appropriate number.
3. Connect the dots.

FIGURE 1-4

Example of Values Balancing

CHAPTER 2

EXPLORING AND ENHANCING YOUR CREATIVITY

COMING ATTRACTIONS:
- One brain, two thinkers
- Mindmapping
- Role of creativity in projects
- Relating values and projects

Everything humankind has invented—
from the wheel to New Age philosophies—
began with our collective creative ability.
And, barring a messiah or a visit from an ET,
all of the advances created in the future—
whether for good or for bad—
will begin with this same creative process.
Understanding and nurturing creative thinking
is one of the most important steps
we can take to improve ourselves and our world.

—MARSH FISHER, CEO, IDEAFISHER SYSTEMS

HOW CREATIVE ARE YOU?

On a scale of 1 (not at all) to 10 (extremely), how would you rate your creativity?

Did you give yourself an 8 or above? Most people don't. Is

that because the world is full of uncreative people? We don't think so, and studies show that the lack of creativity isn't the problem. Many years ago, George Land, author of *Grow or Die,* did a study for NASA which showed that 97 percent of a group of five-year-olds were highly creative. When this same group was evaluated several years later, the number had dropped to 30 percent, and by the time this group reached adulthood, only 2 percent were considered highly creative. Where did the creativity go?

Creativity doesn't just leak away; it gets buried. Buried by years of looking for the one right answer in school, by hundreds of multiple choice tests and rigid lesson plans; buried by boring jobs, workplace politics, restrictive rules and regulations, bureaucratic policies and procedures, and fear of failure, and it gets buried by our own self-definition of "noncreative."

We don't need to learn how to be creative; we need to *unlearn* how to be *uncreative!*

Part of this unlearning process is understanding more about how our brain works and how our education system and our work environment teach us to be less creative than we were designed to be. Once we understand more about our brain, we can begin to use new techniques and tools that will allow our natural creativity to flourish. Think about the following situation:

> You're attending a one-day seminar taught by a friend. It should be a low-key, pleasant day and you're looking forward to it. When you reach the registration desk, however, the coordinator pulls you aside in a panic. The seminar is supposed to start in two minutes, but the instructor has been delayed in traffic. They want to know if you can do a five-minute presentation to get the class going until the instructor arrives. The subject of the presentation is "time."
>
> Think about how you would organize this presentation if you were caught in this situation.

Your first reaction might be a case of palpitating butterflies. The second, probably, would be to grab a pen and paper and try to organize your thoughts. Most people would do this in one of two ways: either they'd just start writing out the presentation, or they'd make a list of points that they wanted to cover. While these are okay ways to organize your thoughts, they use only half of your brain! What you really need is a quick way to get your entire brain working effectively. Later in this chapter we will show you such a tool. But first it's important to know a little more about how your brain works.

ONE BRAIN, TWO THINKERS

A series of studies conducted in the 1960s revealed that certain sets of traits are handled primarily by the different brain hemispheres. These studies, known as the right brain–left brain studies, revealed a great deal about how we think. Until that time, we regarded "thinking" as rational, logical thought processes. Intuition, emotion, visualization, and other "nonlogical" processes were considered nonessential functions that just came along with being human; they were seen as interesting but not particularly productive.

The right brain–left brain studies opened the door to thinking about the brain in a different way. One other major development also changed our concept of our brain: computer technology. As computers became faster and faster, people expected them to outprocess the human brain. And in performing logical processes such as mathematical functions, that was true. However, humans can do some things that even the most powerful computers cannot do. For instance, if you meet your best high school friend at a reunion twenty-five years later, chances are you will recognize him even though he might look a great deal different than he did as a teenager. People can recognize faces, bits of music, complex chess patterns, and the wordplay that makes up much of our humor far better than computers can—at least presently. This ability to recognize patterns, even when they're somewhat distorted, is a critical element of our thinking ability.

The brain is more than a computer.

It's almost as if there are two thinkers inside our heads. One is the logical, rational thinker (sometimes called the left brain), and the other is the pattern-recognizing thinker (referred to as the right brain). We like to call them the Editor and the Generator. Each has its own specific skills and its preferred thinking environments. Here's a summary description of each thinker:

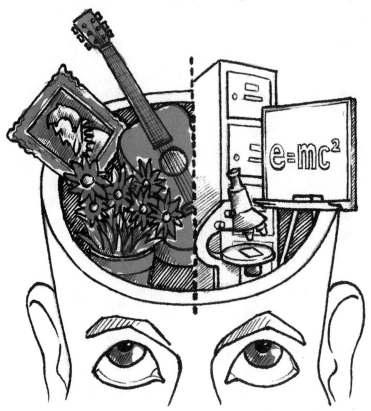

FIGURE 2-1
Brain

The Editor	The Generator
Logical	Intuitive, emotional
Sequential (1, 2, 3)	Leaps (1, 2, red, salmon, N,
Verbal	shoe)
Incremental (sum of parts equals	Visual
whole)	"Groks" (recognizes patterns
Linear	all at once)
Past-oriented	Spatial
	Future-oriented

Specialties

Mathematics	Art
Organization	Imagination
Analysis	Synthesis
Verbal communication	Imagery
Details	Big picture

Preferred Thinking Environment

Data-rich	Color, music, toys
Structure, order	Chaotic, messy
Feedback-rich	Permissive, no negative
Detailed instructions	feedback
Control, decision authority	Seeing the big picture
Individual analysis	Exploring randomly
	Interaction and idea
	sharing

CREATIVITY IS WHOLE-BRAINED

Enhancing our creativity depends on our ability to use both thinkers in the proper sequence. Creativity requires both thinkers ... but they don't think well together. They really don't even like to be in the same room at the same time! The

Generator is extremely sensitive to criticism and, at the slightest hint of judgment, will run and hide. So the first step in enhancing your creativity is to separate the idea-generating stage from the editing process.

First generate, then edit.

Create a thinking space that will thrill the Generator—a space that has color, music, toys, gizmos, visually interesting patterns, and absolutely no negative comments. Spend some time stimulating ideas regardless of whether or not they sound ridiculous. As a matter of fact, force yourself to think of some really off-the-wall ideas. Write them down and just let them be there. Remember this is the Generator's time. The Editor's turn comes next.

Once you have lots of ideas, turn to your Editor for help. Let the Editor sort, evaluate, criticize, gather data, analyze, and make decisions. Working together in this fashion, the Generator and the Editor will enhance your thinking processes and your creativity.

Once you have your two thinkers working together in the proper sequence, it's important to understand where your raw material comes from. You have only one source of creativity— your own unique talents, skills, perspectives, and experiences. You can't be creative with someone else's stuff, because creativity, by definition, is the process of translating who you are into some outward manifestation. It doesn't matter whether that is a painting, an ad campaign, a holiday dinner, a business report, or the raising of a healthy child. The creative process can be applied to all of our activities, eventually yielding a truly creative life.

⌘ ***Ponder Point:*** *Think about a time when you felt truly creative. What were you doing? How did it feel?*

THE ROLE OF CREATIVITY IN PROJECT MANAGEMENT

So what does all this have to do with project management? Everything.

Projects provide you with an opportunity to be creative, to turn ideas based on your values into outward reality. However, many people come up with great ideas but have difficulty managing all the details needed to complete the implementation of those ideas. Others are terrific at managing details but lose track of the big picture or manage details on a not-very-good idea. In order to be an effective project manager, it's important to know how to use both of your thinkers effectively, and it helps to have some good tools.

Good idea plus good implementation equals success.

⌘ ***Ponder Point:*** *Have you worked on projects where creativity was not stimulated or encouraged? What happened?*

MINDMAPPING: A GREAT CREATIVE PROJECT MANAGEMENT TOOL

At the beginning of a project, you need a way to quickly generate ideas and get a big picture of the project. At this point an inherent organizational structure is sometimes apparent, but not always. The perfect tool for the beginning of a project is one that helps stimulate ideas and an understanding of the entire project while allowing any apparent organization to be perceived. Forcing organization at this early stage can turn off the Generator and stifle ideas.

Mindmapping is the perfect technique for this first stage of project management. It is a visual, free-flowing way to capture ideas and map the entire project quickly. It can be compared to a nonlinear method of outlining. (Unlike outlining, however, mindmapping is never wrong!)

Mindmapping is *never* wrong.

Although extremely simple to learn and use, this technique is incredibly powerful because it works the way your brain works. Studies show that the brain works best in five- to seven-minute bursts (although the studies don't tell us how many of those bursts we get per day—some days obviously fewer than others). Mindmapping takes advantage of those bursts by allowing us to capture an incredible amount of information and ideas in a few short minutes. Most individual mindmapping sessions take ten minutes or less, and group sessions seldom last longer than thirty minutes.

Mindmapping effectively engages both sides of the brain and allows us to quickly capture enough information to trigger a pattern. It becomes a form of brain shorthand. Here's a quick overview of how to do mindmapping. There are only two rules:

1. There are no bad ideas.
2. There are no wrong mindmaps.

MINDMAPPING IN EIGHT EASY STEPS

1. *Lighten up!* Let go of the idea of finding a cure for cancer, ending hunger, solving the problem, or writing a report that your boss will love. Mindmapping is simply a brain-dumping process that helps stimulate new ideas and connections. Start with an open, playful attitude. Your Editor can always get serious later.
2. *Think fast.* Your brain works best in bursts, so capture that explosion of ideas as rapidly as possible. Key words, symbols, and images provide a mental shorthand to help you record ideas as quickly as possible.

3. *Judge not.* Write down everything that comes to mind even if it is completely unrelated to the project at hand. If you're brainstorming ideas for a report on the status of carrots in Texas and you suddenly remember you need to pick up your dry cleaning, write down "Cleaning." Otherwise your mind will get stuck like a needle on a record in that "cleaning" groove and you'll never generate those great ideas.

4. *Break boundaries.* Break through the 8½-by-11 mentality that says you have to write on white letter-size paper with black ink or pencil. Use ledger paper or easel paper, or cover an entire wall with butcher paper. The bigger the paper, the more ideas you'll have. Use wild colors, fat colored markers, crayons, or skinny felt-tipped pens. You haven't lived until you've mindmapped a business report with hot pink and Day-Glo orange crayons.

5. *Center first.* Our linear, left-brain education system, at least in Western cultures, has taught us to start in the upper left-hand corner of a page. However, that's not the way the brain works.

⌘ ***Ponder Point:*** *Just for a second close your eyes and visualize an apple on your mind's screen. See it in as much detail as possible—the size, the color, the shape, everything. Now . . . where did you see the apple? At the top left-hand corner? Top right-hand corner? Most people see it in the center of their mental screen.*

Our mind focuses on the center, so mindmapping begins in the middle of the page with a word or image that symbolizes what you want to think about.

6. *Free-associate.* As ideas emerge, print one- or two-word descriptions of the ideas on lines branching out

from the central focus. Allow the ideas to expand out-ward into branches and sub-branches. If an idea is re-lated to a previous one, put it on a sub-branch. If it's not related, start a new branch. Put down all ideas without judgment or evaluation.

7. *Keep moving.* Keep your hand moving. If ideas slow down, draw empty lines, and watch your brain automat-ically find ideas to put on them. Or change colors to reen-ergize your mind. Stand up and mindmap on an easel pad to generate even more energy. Studies show that the big-ger the paper, the more ideas you will generate, and standing up creates more idea energy than sitting down.

8. *Allow organization.* Sometimes you see relationships and connections immediately and you can add sub-branches to a main idea. Sometimes you don't, so you just connect the ideas to the central focus. Organization can always come later; the first requirement is to get the ideas out of your head and onto the paper.

USES FOR MINDMAPPING

- Organizing information and ideas for reports, memos, letters, novels, or poems
- "To do" lists
- Preparing and giving presentations
- Decision-making
- Brainstorming challenges and solutions
- Values clarification
- Meeting agendas and reports
- Project definitions
- Managing projects
- Task analysis
- Grocery lists
- Vacation planning
- Journal entries
- Note taking and chapter summaries

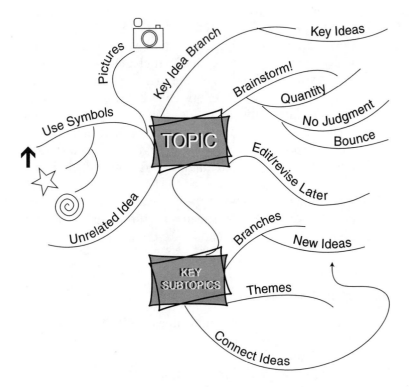

FIGURE 2-2
Example: How to Mindmap

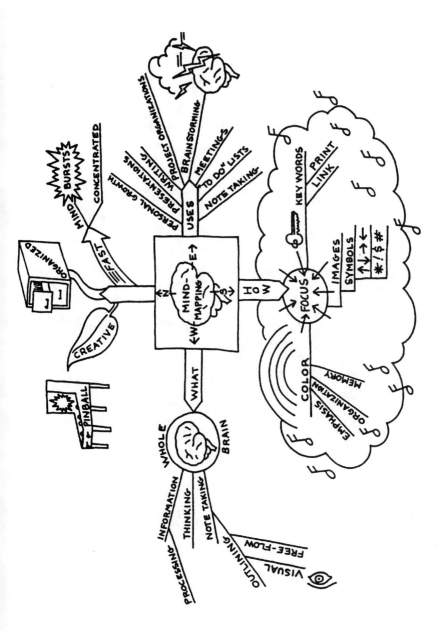

FIGURE 2-3
Example from *Mindmapping Your Personal Guide to Exploring Creativity and Problem-Solving* (Berkley, 1991)

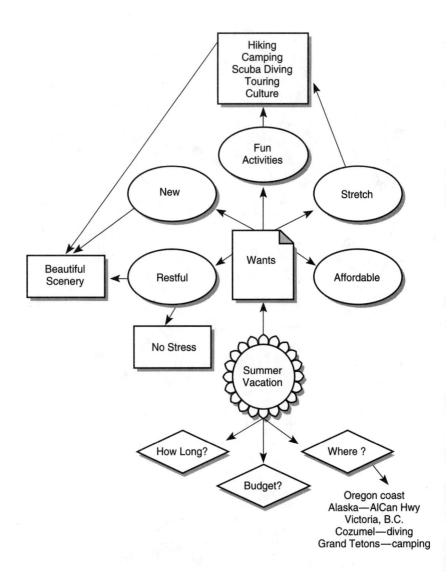

FIGURE 2-4
Example: Summer Vacation Mindmap

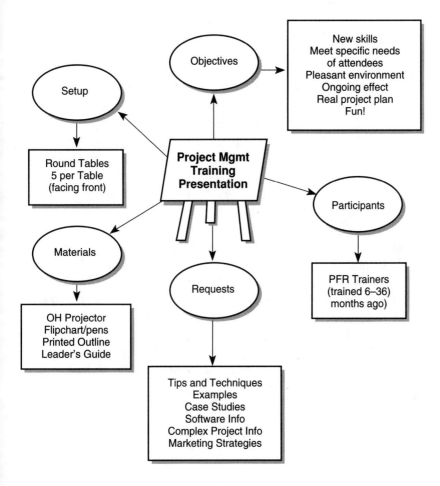

FIGURE 2-5
Example: Training Project Mindmap

In other words, mindmapping is an excellent tool for anything that deals with people, ideas, information, problems, or opportunities. That doesn't leave much out, does it?

The previous pages show several mindmap examples. Figures 2-4 and 2-5 were done with Inspiration, a software program that is excellent for complex mindmaps.

Now it's time for you to try mindmapping. Take a sheet of paper and in a circle in the center, write "My Projects." Then begin to map all of the personal and professional projects you'd like to get done now and in the future. Don't worry about time or resources; just write down everything you would like to accomplish, from cleaning the closet to revamping the personnel policy manual to setting up a new office filing system to creating a new ad campaign. Spend five to ten minutes on this map.

Now look back at your values map (Figure 1-1) and relate each project to one or more of your values. If you find a project that doesn't relate to one of your values, perhaps it's not a project you really want to do, or maybe you left an important value out of your values map. Relating your projects and your values is a critical step in project completion, as it gives you a way to prioritize your projects.

In the next chapter, we're going to put values, creativity, and projects together into a process model that will help you effectively manage any project.

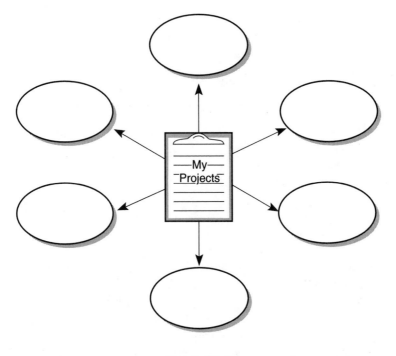

FIGURE 2-6
My Projects Mindmap

CHAPTER 3

BUILDING SUCCESS WITH THE PRODUCTIVITY PYRAMID

COMING ATTRACTIONS:
- Defining success
- Productivity Pyramid

Think big. . . . Set goals. . . . Visualize success.
Do more with less.
Just do it!

But what is "it"? Set *what* goals? Visualize *what* success?

In our society we tend to equate success with material well-being and accomplishments. Big houses, shiny cars, powerful titles, and brave feats provide the most visible signs of success. And there's nothing wrong with striving for those symbols of achievement . . . as long as they're what you really want and not what you think you should want or what you think you need to be happy.

Several years ago, Joyce participated in a Sierra Club backpacking trip into the Golden Trout Wilderness in California's Eastern Sierras. It's a magic place of gentle meadows, rugged peaks, and clear, icy lakes filled with wily trout that are definitely not threatened by the average fisherman. For a good many members of the crew that made this trip, success was defined by peak-bagging, hiking to the top of as many peaks as possible during the trip. Peak-bagging is a fine, healthy activity, but the group didn't seem to have any other definitions of success, which left several of the mountain couch potatoes feeling left out and less worthy.

Similarly, life can leave us feeling left out unless we understand our values and how to translate them into goals that are meaningful to us. What good does it do to think big if what we're really interested in and really value is our relationships with our families and friends? Why should we keep pushing to "do more with less" when what we really want is just to do less?

Time management, as most people perceive it, is trying to get more done each day. The technique we're about to share with you builds on the values you identified in the first chapter and shows you how to accomplish what you care about most.

⌘ ***Ponder Point:*** *Think about your number one governing value. How do you define success for that value?*

PRODUCTIVITY PYRAMID

The Productivity Pyramid, developed by Franklin Covey, is a way to match your values and principles with long-range and intermediate goals and the tasks required to reach those goals. The pyramid represents our approach to life. At its base are our values, those qualities that we care most about in our lives. Goals that are based on our values stimulate our enthusiasm, passion, commitment, and persistence. We are therefore more likely to achieve those goals than objectives that excite less of our passion. Basing our goals and objectives on our values makes it easier to achieve the results we want.

By centering our actions around our values, our time management efforts become the method for implementing our life plan more effectively. Rather than focusing exclusively on our day-to-day activities, we create the foundation of values first.

This foundation means the difference between a meaningful, proactive life built on the things we really want, and an accidental life driven by whims and happenstance.

ELEMENTS OF THE PRODUCTIVITY PYRAMID _____

Values: *Why* we do what we do
Long-range goals: *What* we want to achieve
Intermediate steps/goals (projects): *How* we achieve our
  goals
Daily activities or tasks: What we do *NOW*

FOUNDATION LEVEL: VALUES—THE *WHY*

After we have developed our values map, we have a better understanding of what we want from life. We know what helps us to survive, thrive, and prosper. As we create the Productivity Pyramid, we build on those values and develop a plan for actualizing each value.

Identifying our life values helps us understand why we do what we do, and as a result, we begin to live more effectively. Living effectively means that everything we do is based on one or more of our values. Eventually we can look at all of our actions and ask ourselves what value is being supported by those actions. We can then continue the actions that are values-based and rethink actions that are not consistent with our values.

⌘ **Ponder Point:** *Think about why you're reading this book. Which of your values is it supporting? If you find it's not related to any of your governing values, feel free to put it aside or pass it along to a friend. This is* your *life, and these are* your *values. If reading this book isn't making your life better by supporting one or more of your values, don't waste any more of your valuable time on it.*

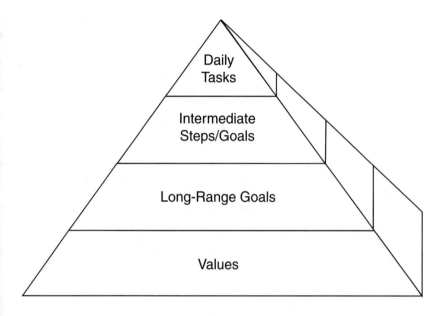

Figure 3-1
Productivity Pyramid

This values clarification process helps us take responsibility for our actions. Sometimes people become reactive and feel as if they are working on a project just because it was assigned to them. This creates a sense of victimization, a feeling of having no control over their actions or destiny. People who get into the victim mode become less effective and take little joy in what they're doing.

Looking at our actions in relation to our values breaks through that victim barrier. For instance, if my boss gave me a project that I had little interest in and that seemed completely unsuitable for me, I might feel that I was being taken advantage of. But she's my boss, so I can't just tell her to take a hike. Taking the victim path, I might grump around, procrastinate, do less than my all, and turn in an inferior result. This path seldom leads to riches, glory, promotions, or satisfaction.

As an alternative, I could take a proactive role. I could look at my values and realize that two of my governing values are financial security and career growth and development. This project offers me an opportunity to do a good job for my boss and possibly strengthen my relationship with her or display talents that have not been recognized previously by the organization. So I jump into the project and make every effort to deliver exactly what my boss wants. This path offers an opportunity to be a rising star.

There is a third possibility. I might realize that the project cannot be reconciled with my values at all. Perhaps my boss wants me to go overseas for six months, but my elderly parents are ill and need my help, and I'm in the last semester of a master's program. I talk to my boss and try to find a different way to meet her needs within the boundaries of my governing values. I demonstrate my concern for the organization's needs while maintaining my personal integrity and balance. If the organization respects individual values, this process should result in an increased understanding and identification of mutually acceptable options. If it doesn't, I'm faced with a difficult choice and may have to find a more values-oriented employer.

What we're looking for is harmony. If we can examine a specific project and recognize how it supports the organization's values as well as our own, we'll be more aligned. Once we recognize this, our level of commitment will be much higher. We can choose an active position rather than a reactive, victim mode. Every project we begin should somehow support one or more of our values or we shouldn't be doing it.

The point of all of this is harmony and inner peace.

Here's an example of how the same project can support both the organization's values and your personal values (Figure 3-2). Assume that your organization has a value of "quality," and one of the ways they support that value is by improving employee performance and skills. Also assume that you have a value of "career growth and development," and to support that value, you look for new projects that will improve your skills and performance.

Enter a new project: Your company decides to offer a new computer training program, and they ask you to develop the program. This is a challenge for you and will require learning new skills, so it supports your career growth value and it supports the company's quality value by improving employee skills. This project is in harmony with the organization's values and with your personal values.

SECOND LEVEL: LONG-RANGE GOALS— THE *WHAT*

The second level of the pyramid is the big picture, the long-range goal, the *what* that we want to accomplish. Each of our life values generally has one or more goals that we believe will enhance it. For instance, one of my goals is to retire at age fifty-five with sufficient savings and investments to allow me to live comfortably. With the help of a financial planner, I determined my long-range goal and the exact amount I needed to save each month to achieve success.

THIRD LEVEL: INTERMEDIATE GOALS— THE *HOW*

Once we have a long-range goal, we need to decide how to get there. This process breaks the long-range goal into intermediate steps. These more manageable pieces, or projects, become the plan for reaching our ultimate objective. One of the intermediate goals related to my retirement objective was to develop an investment portfolio. A project was initiated to determine the best way to achieve this objective, and then to implement it by setting up the necessary accounts such as 401Ks, IRAs, savings accounts, and brokerage accounts.

Organizational

- Daily Tasks
- Computer Training Project
- Improve Employee Performance/Skills
- Quality

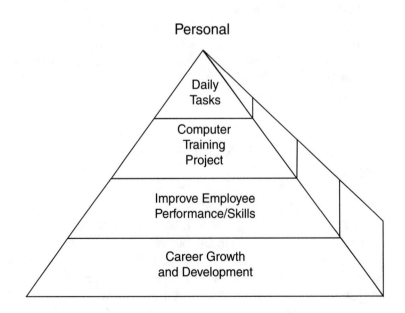

Personal

- Daily Tasks
- Computer Training Project
- Improve Employee Performance/Skills
- Career Growth and Development

FIGURE 3-2
Pyramid Examples

FOURTH LEVEL: DAILY TASKS—THE *NOW*

After we have defined the intermediate goals and projects, we can break them down into daily tasks such as completing the application form for a savings account, arranging for automatic payroll deductions, and so on. When I worked through this process for my value of financial security, it became clear to me that for the remainder of my working career, I needed to maximize my monthly contribution to my 401K plan.

Working backward from my value helped me identify a long-range goal that was then broken down into intermediate goals or projects, which were then translated into daily activities. Following the Productivity Pyramid process gave me a way to create a step-by-step plan, where each step supported my life plan.

Here are some additional examples of the Productivity Pyramid:

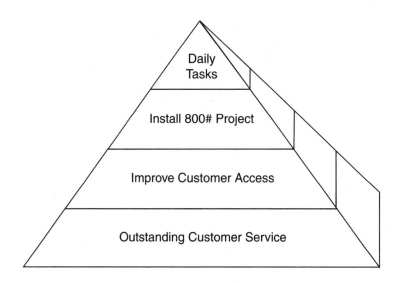

FIGURE 3-3
Pyramid Example: Organizational Value

In the organizational example shown in Figure 3-3, the organization is committed to outstanding customer service (value) and wants to make it easier for customers to report problems (long-range goal). The company decides to install an 800 number for service problems (intermediate goal). It then sets up a project team to plan and implement that goal (tasks).

In the individual example seen in Figure 3-4, this person is committed to developing professionally (value) and has determined that a three-year professional certification process is needed (long-range goal). The first step is to attend a basic training program in another city (intermediate goal), which involves registration, travel, taking time off from work, arranging for pet care, and so forth (tasks).

FIGURE 3-4
Pyramid Example: Personal Value

ONE PYRAMID FITS ALL

The Productivity Pyramid makes any project more effective, from tiny projects to megaprojects such as Boeing's latest airplane, the 777. When Boeing began to think about building the largest and most complex plane ever designed, the company developed a new set of values, which led to a unique set of long-range objectives. These objectives were broken down into a massive set of intertwined intermediate objectives (projects) and individual tasks. The project involved a development budget of $6 billion, over ten thousand people, and more than 3 million parts.

Boeing's vision was to create a top-quality aircraft for profit in an environment of no secrets and no rivalry within Boeing or in its relationship with its customers and contractors. The new value of no secrets and no rivalry was clarified in the following statements:

- Use a new style of management unheard of in the industry: working together while building trust, honesty, and integrity.
- In the past, people were afraid to state a problem because of the practice of killing the messenger. We will instead celebrate our problems and get them out into the open so we can work on them.
- We must come with no limitations in our mind. We must have a shared thought, vision, appreciation, and understanding of what we are going to accomplish together.

Boeing's long-range goals for this airplane were stated as follows:

- Design, develop, and produce a plane safer and more reliable than any other plane in aviation history that is state-of-the-art and service-ready on delivery, to be called the 777.

- Design, develop, and produce a program to empower a massive team of people to implement the "working together" philosophy while creating the 777.

The results of this project were impressive. It came in under budget and was delivered before its due date. The profitability was beyond expectations, it positively changed the management-teamwork paradigm, and it is proving to be a plane that anticipates the changing air travel patterns for the next century.

FOCUSING ON WHAT'S IMPORTANT

The Productivity Pyramid provides a model for making decisions and taking action and keeps us focused on what's important to us. It's a necessary step to begin living our lives with purpose instead of by accident. Too often we live in a reactive mode. We take whatever comes along, waiting for the next great thing, counting on luck, and dreaming about winning the lottery. That creates a victim mentality when things don't drop out of the sky the way we want them to. We look at other people's lives and think, "They're so lucky!" Luck really has little to do with it, yet many, many people live their lives just waiting for good fortune to happen along their way.

Luck = preparation meeting opportunity

Most successful people pay luck due respect but know that most "luck" comes when preparation meets opportunity. The Productivity Pyramid gives us a way to look at what matters and then to create a life plan that prepares us for when opportunity knocks.

Without the clarity that comes with having developed a Productivity Pyramid, when opportunity knocks, we may not recognize it. Not long after I joined Franklin Quest, I was offered a company position in a completely different area. I wasn't sure it made sense for me to take it because it didn't seem to be on my path. It was a tough decision until I looked beyond the short run to my governing values. Then I realized that the move made perfect sense. It was clearly in harmony with my values, and in the long run it was the logical next step for me.

The Productivity Pyramid answers the questions "Why?" (values), "What?" (long-range goals), "How?" (intermediate goals and projects), and "What to do now?" (daily tasks). Many times when we first do this exercise, we find that our lives don't look exactly like our list of values. Rather than feel frustrated, we realize that we now have a road map that guides us toward the life we want. We can look at the list and ask, "How can I bring my life in line with my values?" We then develop a step-by-step plan for achievement. Our list helps us keep the big picture in mind while we work on our projects.

By getting caught up in day-to-day details, we sometimes lose sight of where we want to be going. In an economy where it often takes two incomes to maintain even an average lifestyle, it is especially important to keep our values in mind. Otherwise, small daily decisions can quickly throw us off-balance. Deciding to work an extra hour or to take work home can become habit-forming and can steal time from other areas of our life that may be just as important or more important than work—family, fitness and health, and community service, for example.

The key is finding balance. If I consistently live in a way that slights any one of my values, I'm out of balance. By definition, governing values are those principles and qualities we care about most. When any one of those governing values is missing or not adequately present, our life is not as rich as it could be; there's an emptiness in us. What I'm trying to do is learn to live a more balanced life. When I get up at 6:00 A.M. every Friday to go out and have bagels and coffee with my son, Seth, it's not only a pleasant opportunity to catch up on the week, it's an important activity that supports my family value. Likewise, taking time to ride my horse is not just a leisure activity, but one that enhances one of my primary values and makes me feel better about life.

Many, many mornings when I got up at 5:30 to work on this book, my motivation and energy were high because I was making time for one of my highest priorities at that time: writing this book. Getting up early was also easier because I knew the book was a project—it was going to end someday.

It's important to remember the nature of projects and the flow of energy they sometimes require of us. We are striving for overall balance. I may face a few weeks or months of demanding work, but when the project is over, things will settle back to a manageable pace. If the pace were to continue and become the norm, I would be setting myself up for burnout.

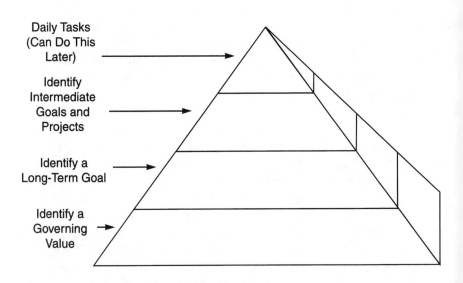

FIGURE 3-5
Exercise: Build Your Pyramid

BUILD YOUR PYRAMID

Complete the blank Productivity Pyramid (Figure 3-5) for several of your values. Don't worry about identifying specific tasks; we'll discuss that part of the process more thoroughly in Section III as we get into managing projects.

ORGANIZING YOUR TIME AND THE FLOOD OF INFORMATION

*Lost, yesterday, somewhere between sunrise and sunset,
two golden hours, each set with sixty diamond minutes.
No reward is offered, for they are gone forever!*

—LYDIA H. SIGOURNEY

TIME FLIES AWAY ALMOST AS fast as information floods in. We spend our days balancing their ebb and flow, our effectiveness caught between these two inevitable forces. We can't stop time or the flow of information, but we can learn to organize and manage them.

The following chapters contain simple, proven techniques for increasing your success through the effective management of time and information flow. If you have these issues under control, you can skim these chapters or simply fast-forward to Section III.

CHAPTER 4

VALUES-BASED TIME MANAGEMENT

The Foundation of Effective Project Completion

COMING ATTRACTIONS:
- Effectively using a day planner
- Daily planning and solitude
- Consistency, consistency

You will never find time for anything.
If you want time, you must make it.

—CHARLES BUXTON

Successful time management is not about getting more done in a day; it's about getting the things done that matter most. Just trying to get more done every day is life in a squirrel cage running faster and faster to nowhere. Getting done what matters most leads to a life of balance, personal satisfaction, and inner peace. Choosing the tasks to be done is more important than any system of completing random tasks. The tasks we manage on a daily basis need to flow up from the pyramid base of our values. If tasks aren't related to our values, why would we devote our time to them?

The choice of *which* tasks is more important than *how* they're done.

The time management system outlined in this chapter is based on the work of Benjamin Franklin, one of the most successful Americans who ever lived and one of the first proponents of time management. Franklin stated, "Dost thou love life? Then do not squander time, for that is the stuff life is made of."

Franklin was an extraordinarily productive person, credited with the creation of the post office, the public library, and many other inventions and personal accomplishments. His productivity was based on more than time management, however. Early in his life, he clarified his personal values and designed a system of focusing on one value each week throughout the year and tracking his progress in a small notebook. His personal autobiography, written when he was in his eighties, details his experiences and his personal successes, crediting many of them to the use of his system.

Many of the activities that flow from our Productivity Pyramid, either individual or organizational, are projects that can be broken down into daily tasks. We will look at the process of managing those projects and tasks in the next several chapters. For now let's focus on time management in general to give us a foundation for getting our day under control before we start to think about managing projects.

THE BASIC TOOL

Some tools are so basic, it's difficult to imagine working without them—the carpenter's hammer, the mechanic's wrench, the cook's knife. While there may be hundreds of variations on these basic tools, the ability to use them effectively is fundamental to mastery of these professions.

It's much the same in today's complex work environment, which requires effective time management, and the fundamental tool is a day planner. This chapter and most of the remaining chapters of the book assume that you are currently using some version of a day planner. If you haven't begun to use one of these "ancillary brains," we suggest that you investigate the many varieties available to you. Later in this chapter we list some of the components you should look for in a good day planner. Regardless of which system you currently use or decide to use, some techniques are recommended in the following pages that will help you customize and enhance this tool's effectiveness.

The day planner is the key to effective time management.

The Franklin Planner has been the key to success for me for the past twelve years. I chose to go to work for Franklin Covey ten years ago because of the day planner; I didn't choose to use their day planner because I worked for them. What impressed me from the very beginning was Franklin Covey's focus on values. This day planner makes it easy for you to stay focused on your values and develop goals and objectives based on those values. However, if you're using another system, that's fine; you can combine the values information in the previous chapters into whatever system you're using.

DAY PLANNER BASICS

Three simple rules will help make your day planner work for you and will greatly enhance your effectiveness and control. Without these basics, your day planner would be just another datebook:

1. **Do it *your* way.** Your day planner is designed to be customized. Make it fit your needs and lifestyle. The more you make it work for you, the more useful it will be.
2. **Use only one calendar.** Throw away all other calendars, especially the one on the fridge and the one on your desk that still shows the joke-of-the-day (or word

or trivia or Ansel Adams photo) from two weeks ago. When everything is in one place, you know where to find it, and nothing slips through the cracks.

3. **Have the day planner with you at all times.** Carry it everywhere. That way you'll never need other calendars, sticky notes, or floating pieces of paper. You won't misplace important information, and you won't have to delay making a commitment until you get back to your home or office to check your calendar.

⌘ *Ponder Point: If you're using a day planner, how long has it been since you've rethought how you use your system?*

COMPONENTS OF AN EFFECTIVE DAY PLANNER

The same day planner that you use for effective time management will become the key to your success in project management. If you are currently using a pocket-size planner, you may want to consider using 8½-by-11-inch project management materials, as they provide more space for the necessary details. The day planner components that are key to project management are as follows:

1. A loose-leaf notebook that will accommodate tabbed divider sheets to be used for projects and other frequently accessed information. Openable rings are essential for customizing your day planner to your specific needs.

2. Daily pages that include a place for (a) a prioritized daily task list; (b) a record-of-events page with space for notes; and (c) a daily appointment schedule.

3. Monthly calendar overview page to see events of the month at a glance.

4. Monthly index to track information in the system.

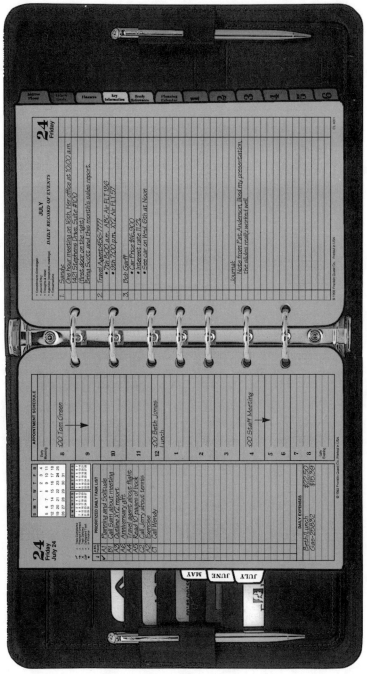

FIGURE 4-1
Day Planner: Daily Format

5. Master task list for those activities you wish to accomplish during the month but have not yet scheduled to a specific day.
6. Address and phone directory.
7. Storage binder.

PRIORITIZED DAILY TASK LIST

This is a "to do" list that reflects priorities based on our values. The problem with a standard "to do" list is that it treats all items on the list as if they were of equal value. This leads to cherry-picking—doing the quickest and easiest tasks so we can check them off. I'm convinced that checking off items on a "to do" list releases endorphins, the powerful brain chemical that causes a feeling of euphoria. If you want proof, answer this question: Have you ever completed a task that wasn't on your list and then written it down just so you could check it off?

Most of the people in my workshops sheepishly answer yes to that question. I consider this proof—a bit unscientific, perhaps, but proof anyway—that checking off items on a list releases feel-good endorphins.☺

Here's an example of a prioritized daily task list (which we will refer to as a "task list" from here on):

24

Friday
July 24

S	M	T	W	T	F	S
			1	2	3	4
5	6	7	8	9	10	11
12	13	14	15	16	17	18
19	20	21	22	23	**24**	25
26	27	28	29	30	31	

✔	=	Task Completed
→	=	Planned Forward
✕	=	Task Deleted
G☞	=	Delegated Task
●	=	In Process

S	M	T	W	T	F	S
	1	2	3	4	5	6
7	8	9	10	11	12	13
14	15	16	17	18	19	20
21	22	23	24	25	26	27
28	29	30				

S	M	T	W	T	F	S
1	2	3	4	5	6	7
8	9	10	11	12	13	14
15	16	17	18	19	20	21
22	23	24	25	26	27	28
29	30	31				

↓	A B C Priority	PRIORITIZED DAILY TASK LIST
✔	A1	Planning and Solitude
	B1	Call Sam about meeting
	A3	Outline XYZ report
	A6	Anniversary gift
	A4	Travel agent about flight
	A5	Read 10 pages of book
	C2	Call Jerry about tennis
	A2	Exercise
	C1	Call Wendy

FIGURE 4-2
A Prioritized Daily Task List

The difference between an ineffective "to do" list and a task list that helps us accomplish our most important objectives is a system of prioritizing. Once the list is made, you need to prioritize each item, labeling it A, B, or C, as follows:

- A's are vital items. They will provide the highest return on investment for your time spent during the day. A's must be completed that day or there will be adverse consequences.
- B's are important items. They should be done that day, but there will be no adverse consequences if the task is not completed.
- C's are optional items that need to be done but are less time-sensitive.

It generally takes only a few seconds to prioritize your tasks after you've made your list. However, the effects of this planning session will be dramatic *if* you don't allow yourself to slip back into the old habit of going for the quick check mark on the fast C item—"call Jean re: tennis," for example. The A's reflect your highest priorities in life; they deserve your time and attention.

ACTION SYMBOLS FOR THE PRIORITIZED DAILY TASK LIST

Here are some symbols that can help you manage your task list on a daily basis. The following symbols should be placed in the far left column of the day planner sheet, next to each task:

- ✔   Check when completed (and collect your endorphin!). ☺

- →   To indicate when an item not done today is forwarded to another day.

- X   Task deleted.

- tdj ◯   To indicate an item that has been delegated to someone else, draw a circle around the status column and write the initials of the person the task was delegated to in the margin.

●   Indicates an item in progress but stalled for the moment. A sign to go on to the next item on the list and come back to this one later. Must be checked or marked with an X or an arrow by the end of the day.

F: Use this symbol to indicate an item that requires follow-up—very helpful for items that have been delegated.

( )   Parentheses mean "refer to." This key symbol allows you to find vital information later. Used in a prioritized daily task list, for example, (4-3) refers you to notes you took in your day planner on April 3.

With this technique, instead of making one "to do" list on Monday and chipping away at it until Friday, you will find that planning become a daily activity that focuses on your highest priorities.

DAILY RECORD OF EVENTS

One of our major everyday challenges is managing a tremendous volume of information. Have you ever done a body search (literally!) to find an important piece of data? You start with a shirt pocket, go to the suit coat pockets, both outside and inside, then search skirt or pants pockets, and finally go through your wallet or purse, looking for that valuable piece of paper with the vital phone number, name, address, or directions, which is now lost. Typically, these floating pieces of paper come out of our pockets at night and sit on the dresser until they go back into our pockets the next day—right up until the day they float away, or are washed away.

No more floating papers!

A daily record-of-events page is the solution to the daily management of information. If you jot down notes on this page from conversations and phone calls, thoughts, and ideas,

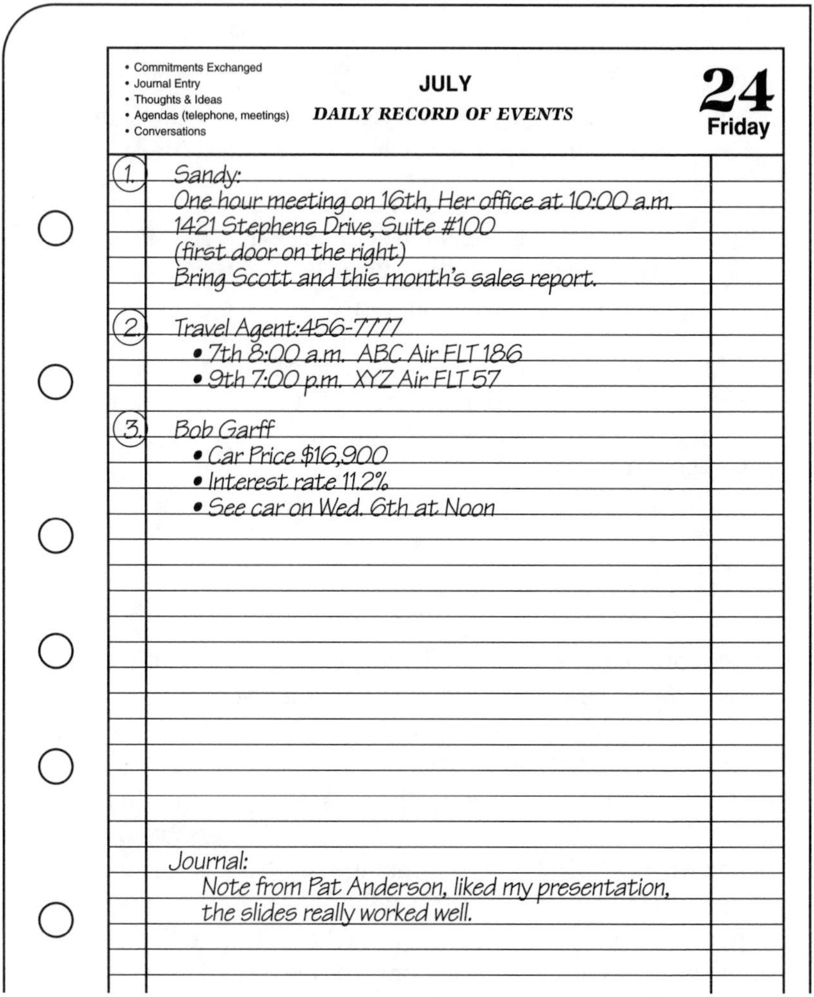

- Commitments Exchanged
- Journal Entry
- Thoughts & Ideas
- Agendas (telephone, meetings)
- Conversations

JULY
DAILY RECORD OF EVENTS

24
Friday

1. Sandy:
   One hour meeting on 16th, Her office at 10:00 a.m.
   1421 Stephens Drive, Suite #100
   (first door on the right.)
   Bring Scott and this month's sales report.

2. Travel Agent: 456-7777
   - 7th 8:00 a.m. ABC Air FLT 186
   - 9th 7:00 p.m. XYZ Air FLT 57

3. Bob Garff
   - Car Price $16,900
   - Interest rate 11.2%
   - See car on Wed. 6th at Noon

Journal:
   Note from Pat Anderson, liked my presentation,
   the slides really worked well.

FIGURE 4-3
Daily Record-of-Events Page

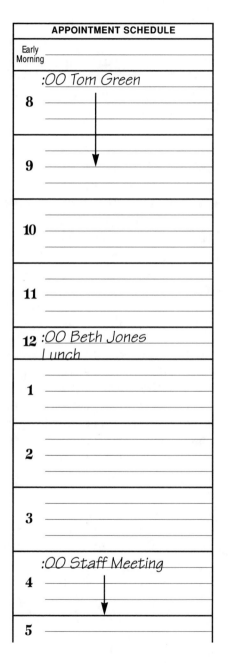

FIGURE 4-4
Daily Appointment Schedule

they are forever saved on the particular day the conversation or activity took place. Later we'll show how the monthly index or monthly calendar provides a retrieval system for any piece of information.

DAILY APPOINTMENT SCHEDULE

The appointment-schedule section is where you keep track of meetings, events, or planned project work sessions. Enter each appointment and block out the necessary time, including preparation and driving time, with an arrow or bar. Once all appointments are entered, you have a visual indicator of how much discretionary time you have left for other daily tasks.

Determine your discretionary time.

Participants in my full-day workshops frequently show me their day planners, and the task list for the day goes all the way to the bottom of the page! This is a classic setup for failure. They have no discretionary time for that day, yet they have a full day's worth of tasks scheduled. Before we can be realistic about how to plan tasks into our day, we need to know how much time is available for their completion.

MONTHLY CALENDAR

This overview of the month serves as a quick reference. In a page-per-day planner system, you generally carry only a few months' worth of the daily pages—typically the current month, the past month, and the coming month. In small planners, generally only the current and preceding months are carried. All other day pages are stored in the storage binder. However, if you carry a year's worth of monthly calendar pages, it will be easy to plan several months into the future. During each day's planning-and-solitude session, you can transfer activities from the monthly calendar to that day's page.

AUGUST

SUN.	MON.	TUES.	WED.	THURS.	FRI.	SAT.
		1	**2**	**3** 9-11: Staff Meeting	**4**	**5**
6	**7** 10-11: Sandy (7-24) 2-4: Training Meeting	**8** 7: Flight (7-14)	**9** 8-4: Meeting San Francisco 9: Flight (7-14)	**10**	**11** 7: Dinner w/Family	**12** 1: Tennis Jerry
13	**14**	**15**	**16** 3-4: Rehearse Presen- tation	**17** 9-11: Staff Meeting (Presen- tation due)	**18**	**19**
20	**21** 12: Lunch w/ Sam	**22**	**23**	**24** 9-11: Staff Meeting 3-5: Closing (7-9)	**25**	**26**
27	**28**	**29**	**30**	**31** 9-11: Staff Meeting		

FIGURE 4-5
Monthly Calendar Page

See the flow of your entire month.

The monthly calendar provides an overview of all appointments, scheduled events, and important dates. At a glance, this calendar will help you see the flow of an entire month. When you need to schedule something, instead of flipping through all of the daily pages, you have just one place to look. The use of the monthly page is simplified and streamlined by the use of parentheses. Not much information is required on this page because all the detail is located on the daily record-of-events page. Simply use a key word—a name or event— and a date in parentheses. This date refers you to the daily page where you have recorded the detailed information regarding the event.

MONTHLY INDEX

After a while, day planners become almost as important for the history they contain as for their future planning function. Questions are always coming up about people you've talked to or tasks you've completed, questions about phone numbers, addresses, costs, and other specifics. Generally we can remember the approximate date of a conversation—last week, last month, last fall—so we start to page through our day planner looking for that bit of information. The monthly index will simplify this process greatly.

Quick reference for important information

At the end of each month, simply page through each day's notes and ask yourself this question: Is there anything on this page that I might need to see again? If there is, make a key word entry on that month's index page. Then, when you begin to look for that elusive bit of information you know is squirreled away in your day planner, you can start with the monthly

INDEX

DATE	Index to important ideas events, thoughts, etc., that have been recorded
1	Tom Green: directions to new office
1	Bob Garff—car information
1	Journal Entry
3	Charles Bennett—new phone number
3	Info on fitness centers
5	Brainstorm—book reading list
8	Kim Smith—H.P. lease terms
9	Bookstore—newly published books
12	Wonderland Travel—Denver reservations
14	Journal entry
15	Copperstate Lease (1) Buyout (2) ITC pass through
18	ACME Bank—mock up on brochure
23	Word-processing catalog list
24	Western Division Convention
30	Highlights—board meeting

FIGURE 4-6
Monthly Index

index. You will usually find what you're looking for at a glance rather than thumbing through all of those daily pages. For example, if on June 17 you had a conversation with a supplier about the cost of file cabinets, you might make a dated index entry that looks like this: file cabinet cost.

Keep the past several monthly indexes with their matching tabbed monthly calendar pages in your day planner. At the end of your calendar year, place all of the index pages in the front of your storage binder to provide a complete index of your entire year.

While some people like to make index entries during the month, I like to review the entire month at once. It takes only ten to fifteen minutes and is a good recap of the month.

An interesting example of how important index pages can be happened to me several years ago. I was living in a duplex, and a new family had just moved in next door. It was a large family with five children, their parents, and a grandparent. When I received my next utility bill, I knew something was wrong because it had quadrupled! I called the power company and asked them to check out the situation. They checked but could find nothing wrong. When I received my next bill, it was still four times higher than normal. Just as a possibility, I decided to turn off the power to my unit and see what happened to the meter. Nothing happened to mine, but my neighbors' meter stopped. I had lived in that unit for ten years and apparently had always been paying the wrong bill. I had never noticed before because our family sizes were approximately the same.

Anyway, I asked the power company to investigate, and they discovered that, indeed, the meters were reversed and I had a $500 refund coming. I waited several weeks for the check, and when I called to check on it, I learned that the woman I'd been working with had left the company and no one knew anything about my problem!

Well, day planner to the rescue. I went back to my monthly indexes, reconstructed the conversations, sent the power company a letter detailing the problem (with a veiled reference to "my lawyer"), and received a check within a week.

MASTER TASK LIST

The master task list page, located at the beginning of each month's daily pages, is a place to record the tasks and goals you want to accomplish during the month that are not yet scheduled for a specific day. As your month unfolds or as a part of your daily planning, check this list and plan for a time when you can accomplish these tasks. Work them into your prioritized daily task list so that by the end of the month you will have them checked off.

ADDRESS AND PHONE DIRECTORY

Part of the value of the day planner is that it is with you always and that it provides you with the information you need. When you are away from your office, you often need address and phone information. Your day planner should contain this information so that you do not have to carry a separate address book.

STORAGE BINDER

Noncurrent daily pages and other data are kept in the storage binder. This should be kept in a place that is accessible to you when you are doing your daily planning, since referring to past information is often part of that planning process. The storage binder makes it possible to carry only current information in your planner.

At the end of the month, after I fill in my monthly index, I take all the daily pages out of my day planner and store them in the time management storage binder. At the same time, I take all other project-related forms out and store them behind the appropriate tabs in my day planner or my project management storage binder. By storing the forms in this way, you set up a system where the information can be easily retrieved.

EXAMPLE OF THE DAY PLANNER PROCESS

During a phone conversation with Sandy, you set up a one-hour meeting in three weeks at 10:00 A.M. In your daily record-of-events you make notes about the date, time, location, and directions. Sandy also asks you to bring Scott and a copy of this month's sales report. While you're on the phone, go to your monthly calendar, confirm that you have that time available, and make the entry shown in Figure 4-5.

This entry lets you know the basics: That on August 16 you have a meeting from 10:00 to 11:00 with Sandy and that the details are recorded in your July 24 record of events. When you need the details, you can flip back to the July 24 daily record-of-events page and see the entry shown in Figure 4-7.

This note also reminds you to call Sam, so you enter that task on your daily task list.

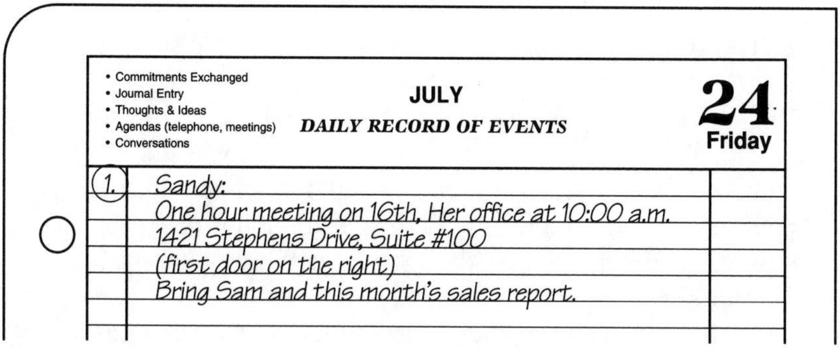

	JULY **24** Friday

- Commitments Exchanged
- Journal Entry
- Thoughts & Ideas
- Agendas (telephone, meetings)
- Conversations

JULY
DAILY RECORD OF EVENTS

24
Friday

1. Sandy:
   One hour meeting on 16th. Her office at 10:00 a.m.
   1421 Stephens Drive, Suite #100
   (first door on the right)
   Bring Sam and this month's sales report.

FIGURE 4-7
Daily Records of Events

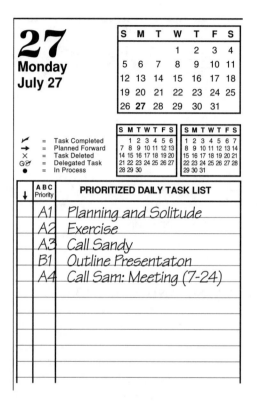

FIGURE 4-8
Prioritized Daily Task List

When you call Sam, you are reminded that the details about the meeting, date, time, location, and directions are located on the July 24 record-of-events page, along with the note that he should bring this month's sales report.

Now, you realize, having worked with Sam in the past, that he not only doesn't use a day planner but he is notorious for forgetting details. You decide that it will be in everyone's best interest if you call and remind Sam the day before the meeting. You go into your planner one day before the meeting and make the following entry into your task list: "F: Sam re Meeting (7-24)."

The F: is a symbol to remind you to follow up on actions or

↓	A B C Priority	PRIORITIZED DAILY TASK LIST
	A1	Planning and Solitude
		F: Sam Re: Meeting (7-24)

FIGURE 4-9
August 16 Prioritized Daily Task List

delegated tasks. This entry lets you know you've talked to
Scott and you're just following up to remind him of the meeting and to bring the sales report.

DAILY PLANNING AND SOLITUDE

Every day your most important task—your A1 priority—
should be planning and solitude. Take ten to fifteen minutes
to plan your day and remind yourself of what's most important
to you in your life. Instead of living each day in a reactive
mode, this planning time will help your day run more
smoothly and help you feel that you are on top of things.
Saying "I don't have time to plan" puts your day in charge of
you rather than you in charge of it!

ENDORPHIN ASIDE—If you do your planning and solitude
first thing every morning, you get to check it off immediately
and start your day with an endorphin!☺

A1: Planning and Solitude—your ten-
minute-a-day gift to yourself

CONSISTENCY, CONSISTENCY, CONSISTENCY

Whenever you do your planning, try to be consistent. The more consistent you are, the more you will form the planning-and-solitude habit, and the more you will see results. Many people like to do their planning at the end of the day before going home so they can get a running start in the morning. I like to do it first thing in the morning. Whatever time you do it, choose a place and time free from interruptions. If I waited until I got to the office to do my planning and solitude, it would never happen. Spending a few minutes privately at home first thing in the morning has been far more effective for me.

Planning—same time, same place

TIP—Make sure the place where you do your planning has all the materials you will need within reach, including your storage binder, which is invaluable for retrieving information from prior months.

It's a good idea to quickly review your personal and business values and goals every day. Without this frequent reminder, it's easy to lose focus and become reactive. This leads us to working on other people's agendas rather than on our own. Here's a summary of the daily planning procedure:

1. Select an environment free from distractions where your storage binder is handy.
2. Review your values and goals.
3. Review the previous day's task list and bring forward any incomplete activities.
4. Review the previous day's record-of-events page and add any tasks that need to be done today.
5. Review the monthly calendar for today's scheduled events and appointments. Bring these forward to today's appointment schedule.

6. Review the master task list for specific activities that need to be done today.
7. Add any other appropriate activities for today to the task list.
8. Review the next few days' schedules to see what needs to be prepared. Add any appropriate tasks.
9. Prioritize today's activities according to what is vital (A), important (B), and optional (C). Analyze your vital tasks and assign an appropriate sequence: A1, A2, A3. Assign numbers to the B's and C's as well.

SAMPLE DAY

1. You start your morning with a planning-and-solitude session as A1 in your day planner, the same way it is in your life every day. As you follow the daily planning procedure, you look at your monthly calendar and realize that this morning you have a meeting with Sandy. As you write this on your appointment schedule for today, you enjoy a moment's peace as you remember yesterday's conversation with Scott. You are confident that he has the sales report ready and will be at the meeting on time. You get your first check mark for the day, and you're ready to continue.
2. While you are preparing for work, a flash of inspiration comes regarding the presentation you are giving next week. You quickly jot it down on the daily record-of-events page. You know that when you review this page during tomorrow morning's planning-and-solitude session, you can incorporate that idea into your presentation notes.
3. As you arrive at the office and begin your day, your next activity, A2, instructs you to prepare for the afternoon training meeting you conduct every month. You refer to

a customized tab in your planner for the notes on this training, revise your plan for the class, and give this task a check mark.

4. "A3—Call Shannon re: trip." You call your friend Shannon, who lives in Portland, tell her you will be in town on business for a day next week, and set up a dinner engagement. She recommends Marco's in Multnomah because it's Thursday night and that's the night they serve their mulligatawny soup special (it's the best!). She gives you directions on how to get there and when to meet. You record all of this under a heading in your daily record-of-events page: "Shannon re: trip to Portland." You also immediately turn to the correct day in your monthly calendar for next Thursday and write "6:30 Dinner w/ Shannon (7-31)," knowing that it will be easy to get back to those directions August 17 when you are ready to leave the business meeting and drive to Multnomah. Another check . . . another endorphin!☺

5. While you are working on your next item, you think of something you need to do the day before the trip, so you flip your daily page to August 16, quickly write down the task, and return to your present task without much of a distraction.

6. During an evening shopping trip to the mall, you find the perfect gift for your son's birthday, but it isn't for two months yet. You decide to buy the present now and hide it until his birthday. You know you have done things like this before and then forgotten where you hid it, so this time, after wrapping and hiding the present, you open your storage binder to the daily page two days before your son's birthday, and record in the task list, "Gift for Seth (linen closet)." And in case it needs to be exchanged for a better fit, you staple or tape the receipt to that day's page.

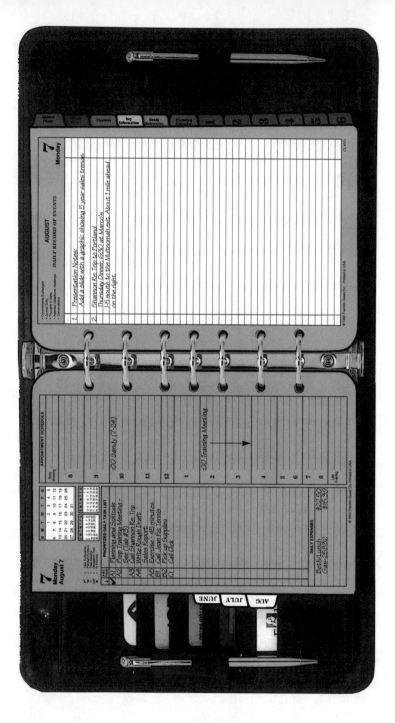

FIGURE 4-10
Sample Day

ONE-MONTH EXPERIMENT

It takes approximately one month to instill a new habit pattern. If you follow this procedure every day for a month, the procedure will go from being a new pattern that requires effort and concentration, to being a daily habit that is smooth and easy. The one-month test period will demonstrate to you the high value of the effects of this system. I assure you that if you follow this process each day for a month, you will see a noticeable improvement in your personal productivity.

Thirty days to a new habit!

Having an effective system for managing our daily lives and activities now becomes the foundation for more effectively managing our projects. Information about significant projects can be set up in a project tab in your day planner. In the next several chapters we will discuss the process and the tools that will help us manage our projects. The idea is to have our project work coordinated so that at any given time we know what work needs to be done and on what projects. That work is coordinated into our day along with other tasks and appointments that are not project-related.

Before we get into the details of managing projects, however, we have one more hurdle to discuss—our desk. The next chapter will show you an easy-to-use but highly effective way to control the information that flows across your desk.

CHAPTER 5

It's Hard to Manage Your Project if You Can't Find Your Desk

COMING ATTRACTIONS:

- Information or action item?
- The Simple as 1-2-3 Desk System
- Rules of paper management
- Time-Activation system
- Radar O'Reilly memory system

Three rules of work:
1. Out of clutter, find simplicity.
2. From discord, find harmony.
3. In the middle of difficulty lies opportunity.

—ALBERT EINSTEIN

Clutter sucks creativity and energy from your brain.

The busier we are, the less time we have for day-to-day office maintenance, and the more we're buried by stacks of papers, an unending pile of stuff to be read, tasks to do, and an ever-growing volume of voice mail and e-mail messages. This overload of information bogs down our creativity and efficiency. Just finding the right piece of paper at the right time becomes a major challenge. Some estimates indicate that we spend as much as six weeks a year looking for stuff!

All of this is compounded by the fact that many of us also have offices at home where we are faced with even more mail, phone calls, faxes, e-mail, and voice mail messages. Fortunately there is a system to help you manage this overload and prevent it from stealing time from your projects and priority activities. The system is called the Simple as 1-2-3 Desk System and it's based on two fundamental ideas:

- In order for any desk-organization system to work, *it must be as simple as throwing stuff on your desk.*
- The world doesn't need a better filing system, it needs a *fail-safe retrieval system.*

The primary principle of this system is that *everything* that comes into your office, regardless of the source, is either trash, information, or an action item, and all of these items can be grouped into three categories—hence "simple as 1-2-3":

1. Trash—junk that can immediately be thrown away
2. Fileables—important information that needs to be read or be filed for future retrieval
3. Action items—details about activities that need to be done

The Simple as 1-2-3 Desk System allows you to quickly and effectively categorize, store, and retrieve all of this incoming material. It is something like an emergency room triage system for information, ensuring that the most important items will be addressed first and nothing will get lost in the shuffle.

SIDEBAR FROM JOYCE: A SYSTEM SIMPLE ENOUGH

Lynne and I have been friends and associates for years, and during those years Lynne has made several efforts to put me on the path to organization. And I *have* made progress. Somewhere along the line I started putting my "to do" items down *before* I finished them. When I first started using my organizer, the list of unfinished items was so intimidating that I'd put things down only after I finished them and could cross them off the list—it was much more gratifying!

But I still belong to the "pile management" mentality. In case you're wondering, I'm not one of those "Yes, but I know where everything is" types. I have spent years looking for missing scraps of papers, lost documents, and ideas that have gone walkabout in the foreign territory of my desk.

So when Lynne talked about adding a chapter on desk management, I smiled politely and cringed inwardly. It wasn't until she told me about James Young and his philosophy—"If the system isn't as easy as dropping stuff on your desk, people won't use it"—that I started to relax. Since I'm an expert at dropping stuff on my desk, I thought maybe, just maybe, this system would work for me. I was a little put off, however, when Lynne said I was our best test case—if it would work for me it would work for anybody.

Lynne: The only reason I said that was because in all of the years we've known each other, I've never been in Joyce's office. . . . Hmmm . . . think that might mean something?

Here's a diagram of the Simple as 1-2-3 Desk System:

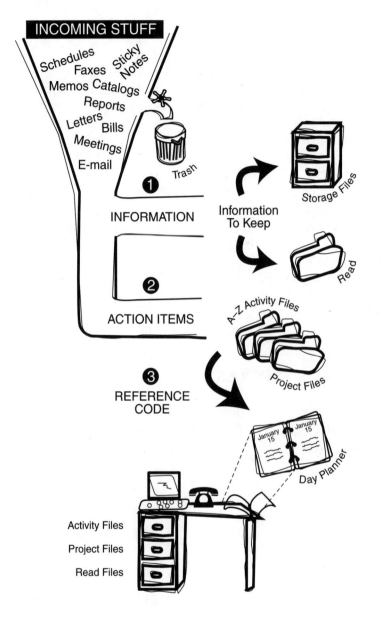

FIGURE 5-1
Simple as 1-2-3 Desk System

The main tool for the Simple as 1-2-3 Desk System is your day planner. It is the control point of the system as it helps you track and manage your action items regardless of source— phone calls, drop-in visits, meetings, e-mail, faxes, and so on. Your day planner is the central processing unit (CPU) for effective management of your new desk system.

While the 1-2-3 Desk System requires an effective filing system, it doesn't matter which system you use. As James Young, one of the system's creators, states, "What the world does *not* need is another filing system, but rather a *fail-safe retrieval system*." You don't have to change your current filing system; this simple desk system will work with the one you have. If you don't have an effective filing system in place, refer to Appendix B, Best-Bet Filing System.

WHAT'S ON YOUR DESK?

Stop for a moment and take a quick inventory of everything on your desk right now. Make check marks next to the items that are currently on your desk.

__Memos
__ Invoices
__ Fax printouts
__ Minutes and information from meetings
__ Project or other files
__ Letters to be answered
__ Schedules
__ Catalogs
__ Budgets
__ Reports
__ Reading material
__ Sticky notes
__ Computer printouts

__ E-mail printouts
__ Notes

RULES FOR PAPER MANAGEMENT

As you try to decide what to do with all this stuff, especially if your stacks are turning into heaps, here are two basic rules to keep in mind:

Rule 1. Never operate your life from a stack of paper, but rather from a prioritized daily task list.

Rule 2. Every remaining piece of paper, after you have sorted out the trash, is either an *action item* to be delegated or time-activated (details later) into your day planner; or *information* to be filed.

Rule #1—Think about what happens when you try to deal with a stack of paper. You take the first piece of paper off the stack, read it over, realize you can't do anything about it right now, and put it back on one corner of your desk. The next item, the same thing. The next item, you do what needs to be done and then realize that you may need the original piece of paper later, so you put it in a different stack on another corner of your desk. You are just rearranging the stacks! It's impossible to prioritize a stack of paper. When you're dealing with a stack, the most important item in that stack may be on the bottom . . . where you may never get to it.

You can't prioritize a stack.

Rule #2—If a piece of paper is both an action item and information, treat it as an action item first. Look at the list of stuff on your own desk and determine whether each item is an action item or information. You will probably notice a pattern: while some items need to be filed or read, most things on your desk are probably action items waiting for you to do something with them.

When James Young teaches a time management workshop, he asks a volunteer to bring everything stacked on his or her desk to the workshop. He then helps the individual go through and organize the materials. At a recent workshop, the volunteer brought a 33-gallon trash bag full of stuff! After sorting through the first several inches of it, it was clear to the owner of the bag, and to everyone else in the class, that after the trash was sorted out, what was left was either an action item or information, and about 95 percent of the items needed an action taken. These made up a large stack reinforcing the importance of rule number one: Never operate your life from a stack of paper, but rather from a prioritized daily task list.

Once we have divided our desktop stuff into action items or information, we can deal with them separately. This chapter will deal primarily with action items; for filing details see Appendix B.

TIME-ACTIVATION SYSTEM

Time Activation is the process of deciding what needs to be done and when in a way that gives you control and confidence that it will be done. To Time-Activate an action item, we need to determine three things:

- *What* needs to be done—task description
- *When* it needs to be done—due date
- *Where* the information is stored—action files

Most action items will be stored in your action files. These are A-to-Z holding files located in the most accessible portion of your desk. Remember the basic idea of this system: if it isn't as easy as throwing stuff on your desk, you probably won't use it. So make it easy for yourself.

The file drawer where your action files are located should contain only three kinds of items:

1. A-to-Z Pendaflex files for anything that requires action
2. Current project files
3. Reading file

Example: You receive a faxed request for a summary report of new clients. You know it will take a couple of hours to prepare, and it is due next Wednesday. You can't get to it until Monday, so you make the following notes:

Time Activation: Day planner location—
                          prioritized daily task list: Monday
                          Entry—new client report (AF-C)

This tells you *what* needs to be done and *where* the task information is stored—in action file C—for "client."

Since this piece of paper needs no activity until Monday and it is safely noted on your daily task list for that day, the fax can be filed away under C, and you don't have to worry about it anymore . . . *or see it on your desk*. You've just *safely* removed a piece of mental and visual clutter.

TIP—Keep an article cutter handy. When you find an article that you want to read, clip it out and put it in your reading file. When you are headed out for a business trip or doctor's appointment, take that file with you.

↓	A B C Priority	PRIORITIZED DAILY TASK LIST
	A1	Planning and Solitude
		New Client Report (AF-C)

FIGURE 5-2
Time-Activate the Client Report

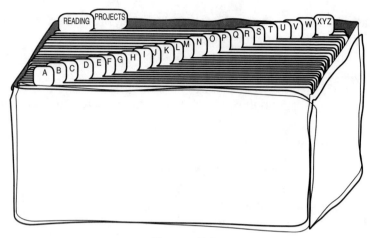

FIGURE 5-3
A-to-Z Activity Files

This system will take care of every piece of paper that represents an action item.

↓	ABC Priority	PRIORITIZED DAILY TASK LIST
	A1	Planning and Solitude
		Jack Denver Ltr: (AF-D)

FIGURE 5-4
Time Activate: Jack Denver Letter

The "AF-D" in parentheses tells you the third part of the Time-Activation process—where the item is stored: in your action file under D, for Denver.

Let's say that the next item in your stack is an invoice to be paid. Decide when this needs to be done, and open your day planner to that day. Your entry might look like this:

↓	ABC Priority	PRIORITIZED DAILY TASK LIST
	A1	Planning and Solitude
		Pay Planning
		Analysts (AF-I)

FIGURE 5-5
Time Activate: Pay Invoice

You then put the invoice in the I file. The reference in parentheses tells you the paperwork is in your action file, under I, for Invoice.

The third item in your stack is a report you need to work on. After deciding when this needs to be done, you enter the following note on the chosen date in your day planner:

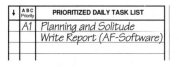

↓	ABC Priority	PRIORITIZED DAILY TASK LIST
	A1	Planning and Solitude
		Write Report (AF-Software)

FIGURE 5-6
Time Activate: Write Report

This indicates that you have a current project file located in your action file drawer labeled "Software." Information for that report is in that file.

SIDEBAR FROM JOYCE: COLOR ME PURPLE

By noon on a normal, hectic day of phone calls, meetings, and errands, I had my action file drawer set up, complete with a full set of purple (my current color) Pendaflex folders. Purple for the A-to-Z files, yellow for projects, and orange for my "read" file. Color is important—if I'm going to do this, I'm going to use the colors I like.

By three o'clock *everything* was off my desk and in the files, and all tasks were logged in my day planner. It's kind of nice to see the wood of my desk for a change. Martha, my office mate and an extremely organized person, questioned how long this would last, and I answered that if it lasted more than two days, it would be a new record.

THE RADAR O'REILLY MEMORY SYSTEM

During one episode of *M*A*S*H*, Radar O'Reilly, the supply clerk, displayed a memory system that provides a lesson for all of us. Radar worked for the colonel, who wanted to find some paperwork related to Jeep maintenance. The conversation went something like this:

"Radar," the colonel asked, "would this paperwork be filed under *J* for Jeep or *M* for maintenance?"

"Neither. It's under *I*," Radar replied as he proudly pulled the document out of the file.

"Radar, why would a document about Jeep maintenance be filed under *I?*" asked the colonel.

"*I* for Iowa," Radar replied matter-of-factly. "We have a lot of Jeeps in Iowa, and every time I think of Iowa, I think of Jeeps."

Now, Radar's system may not be the best for an office filing system where everyone might think of something different when they think of Iowa, but it's perfect for *your* action files, where you want a *fail-safe retrieval system*. When you place an item in your action files, ask yourself, "What trigger word will I always associate with this document?" Then file that document in the action file beginning with the first letter of that word, and that letter becomes the pointer back to the document. For Radar, a Jeep action item would be filed under *I,* and the day planner pointer would be "AF-I," for action file *I*.

Day planner pointers equal fail-safe retrieval.

TAMING THE SECOND BEAST

Two beasts play havoc with our desk and our time management. The first is the paper beast, but the Simple as 1-2-3 Desk System, explained above, shows you how you can control the paper in your life. The other beast can be even more insidious: it's the non-paper beast—that increasing flood of information and activities that comes your way by telephone, voice mail, meetings, drop-in visitors, whiteboard brainstorming sessions, conferences, and hallway encounters.

The first step in controlling this beast is to capture it on paper. Most of us know this step, so our desk becomes a mass of sticky notes, yellow legal pad sheets, napkins, and other scraps of paper that often fall into a cosmic black hole never to be seen again.

Information records control informal oral information.

There is a better way—information records. This is simply a set of A-to-Z tabs for your day planner (and a corresponding set for your storage binder for completed forms). Blank sheets of day planner paper or specialized information record sheets are used to capture the non-paper action item information. The fail-safe retrieval system is the A–Z tabs in your day planner. Basically, this works like a set of mini–action files. Here is an example:

While passing in the hall, your boss asks you to prepare a list of possible vendors for a new software system for Thursday's meeting. When you get back to your desk, you enter the details on an information record sheet, making notes about all the specifics your boss asked for. Then, after Time-Activating the action item, you store this sheet in your information record A-to-Z tabs.

This is a simple project that just involves pulling together information you already have, so it can be done in a few minutes on Wednesday. Your daily task list entry would look like this: "Wednesday—vendor list (IR-J)." This tells you *what* (vendor list), *when* (Wednesday), and *where* the information is stored (information record tab *J* because your boss's name is Steve Jones). This is an ongoing record because of your frequent interactions (see Figure 5-7).

I keep an information record page dedicated to each of the people, subjects, and groups that I communicate with on an

1. Complete the contact information at the top of the form.

2. Date the entries.

3. Use columns to record information and notes: left column equals "I said"; right column equals "He said."

4. Flag items that require follow-up. Record status check marks or other valuable information about the contact type. For example, VM for voice mail, # for phone conversation, and IP for an in-person conversation.

5. Time Activate or record any follow-up needed on the appropriate day's prioritized daily task list or appointment schedule.

6. File the information record alphabetically by name, organization, or subject in your planner's A–Z file tabs.

7. As pages are completed, store them in a corresponding A–Z index set in your storage binder.

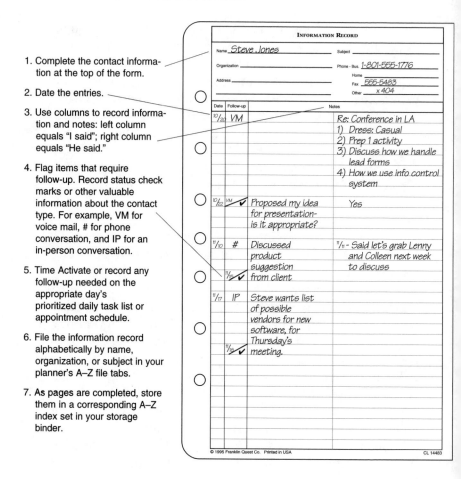

FIGURE 5-7
Information Record

ongoing basis. If I get a phone call or voice mail related to one of those, I turn to the appropriate information record page and immediately have a record of prior conversations and action items. This may take a nanosecond longer than writing something on your daily record-of-events page, but it pays big dividends as it refreshes your memory about the status of the communication and eliminates worrying about losing those little scraps of paper.

If you use an information record form such as the one shown in Figure 5-7, you are provided with a place to list the person, group name, or subject at the top with a phone number and address. This form is stored behind the alpha tab corresponding to the last name of the contact, group, or subject. The form tracks the first-person conversation ("I said") in one column, and the reply ("he or she said") in the other. This provides not only a reminder of information you need to discuss but also written documentation of the reply or outcome and creates a complete history of the contact. Future follow-up can be noted as necessary.

It is only necessary to carry the current pages of the information record with you in your day planner. Overflow forms can be kept in a storage binder marked "Information Records" and filed in a duplicate set of A-to-Z tabs. This storage binder should be the same size as your day planner so that completed pages can be easily transferred.

SIDEBAR FROM JOYCE: WHAT'S THIS?

An amazing thing happened today! It's day five of this new system and there's still nothing on my desk except my day planner, my phone, and some toys. But that's not the amazing part. Today at 4:15 I *finished* my task list! Everything on my list was done, plus I had responded to a rush request for a proposal and was still done before 5:00. Talk about an endorphin rush!

Lynne quotes a statistic that says the average person spends *six weeks* a year looking for stuff. Maybe that's what's happening. I haven't looked for anything in the past four days. Maybe all that time is going into productive stuff. This is scary!

SPECIFIC IDEAS FOR HANDLING PHONE CALLS, VOICE MAIL, AND ELECTRONIC MAIL

It's important to remember that phone calls, voice mail, and e-mail can be categorized as information or action items. Here are some specific tips for handling these non-paper communications.

Take short notes on information record sheets or on daily record-of-events pages.

Phone Calls and Voice Mail

Even people with the best memories can seldom recall all important data from a phone call days, weeks, or even months later, when it may still be important. Regardless of whether you are listening to a live phone call or to voice mail, there may be information that needs to be recorded and activities that need to be done. Jotting notes on your daily record-of-events page regarding the highlights and important information from the conversation will give you documentation you can retrieve as needed.

For those people I communicate with on an ongoing basis, I turn to their page in the information record section of my day planner. Note-taking is a skill that improves with practice, but the key is to keep it quick and brief and to record only the important information.

Abbreviating is also very helpful. After a while you can create your own form of shorthand. When I listen to voice mail, I put a heading on the page, "VM," and the number of messages indicated by the system—"VM: 10," for example. Then I know the next several entries were written from voice mail messages. When taking notes on a live conversation, it is helpful to put a notation by that entry that denotes a phone call, as opposed to a voice mail message. A number sign (#), for example, can denote a telephone conversation.

As soon as any conversation results in an action item, enter a note on your prioritized daily task list briefly describing the task. An arrow in the parentheses pointing to the right will indicate that the additional information needed about this task is noted on the daily record-of-events page. (See Figure 5-8.)

E-Mail

As with other communication sources, e-mail can result in trash, information, or action items; therefore the Time-Activation system works in the same way. With the growing number of discussion lists, the majority of e-mail is probably trash—stuff that is more or less interesting but does not result in information that needs to be filed or acted upon. Delete those items immediately. What is left is either information or action items. If it is information, choose your filing medium—electronic or paper. E-mail can be saved in computer files that are set up with descriptive directory names and filenames, or it can be printed out and stored like other paper information.

Because it is so easy to respond to e-mail messages, it is best to take care of simple requests immediately. You may have a specific time set up each day to handle your e-mail. Reply as quickly and succinctly as possible, send it, and be done. If the action item involves more time and resources than a quick reply, Time-Activate it into your day planner so that it comes up at the appropriate time. Use your task reference to refer you to your e-mail system, to an electronic folder, or to a printout stored in your action item file.

PRIORITIZING NEW ACTION ITEMS

Often action items come up during the day that were unforeseen during your morning planning and solitude session. Sometimes they are high priority and need to be scheduled

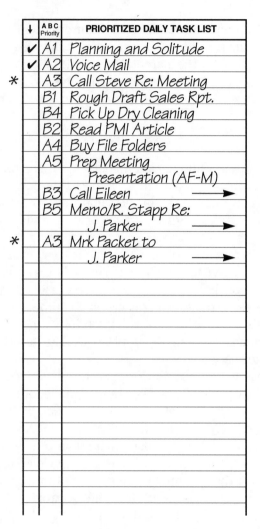

↓	A B C Priority	PRIORITIZED DAILY TASK LIST
✔	A1	Planning and Solitude
✔	A2	Voice Mail
*	A3	Call Steve Re: Meeting
	B1	Rough Draft Sales Rpt.
	B4	Pick Up Dry Cleaning
	B2	Read PMI Article
	A4	Buy File Folders
	A5	Prep Meeting
		Presentation (AF-M)
	B3	Call Eileen ⟶
	B5	Memo/R. Stapp Re:
		J. Parker ⟶
*	A3	Mrk Packet to
		J. Parker ⟶

FIGURE 5-8
Reprioritizing During the Day

into your already planned day. Here's an example of two items that came in during a typical day and were recorded on the daily record-of-events page of my day planner:

Eileen: Left msg. re: new information retrieval syst. to be taught in seminars. Has ??'s re: coord. w/ old system. Call today, if possible.

John Parker: Inq. re: pm training in their org. (address & phone #) I will send info today and refer to their local AE (Rick Stapp).

Since these new items came in during the day after my original planning and solitude session in the morning, they needed to be prioritized in relation to the other things I already needed to do that day. Of the new items, "Call Eileen" and "Call Rick" are both priority B, because calling them sometime within the next two days is okay. The marketing packet to be sent to the client today, however, is of vital importance and must be done today.

Since A1 (planning and solitude) and A2 (answer voice mail) are scheduled first thing every day—Monday through Friday, at least—I give this new task a priority of A3. I already have an A3 on today's list, however, so I put an asterisk in the margin by the original A3 (see Figure 5-8). I now know that before I take care of this original A3, I have a new A3 that needs to be taken care of first. This way, no matter what new tasks come into my day, I am coordinating them with my other priorities. This reflects the realities of my day and the fact that my original plan for the day will be influenced as other events come into my day.

SIDEBAR FROM JOYCE: STILL GOING . . .

The funniest thing happened today—someone asked *me* about my desk organization system! It has been a month since I started the Time-Activation system. My desk is still clean, projects are under control, and I've quit worrying about loose ends (at least as much as I used to). I know where to find stuff, and I'm getting more work done.

One friend, who happened to be around at the beginning of this project, has been keeping a close eye on my desk, probably waiting for it to collapse into its former state of pile chaos. Today he finally asked for the details of the system. Maybe I'll keep it a secret.

Once you have a comfortable system for managing your time and the information and activities that flow across your desk, you're ready to incorporate your projects into that system. The next chapter gives you an overview of a process for managing projects more effectively.

Special thanks to James Young who collaborated extensively on this chapter.

DOING AND *DONE!*

MAKING PROJECT COMPLETION EASY

C O M I N G   A T T R A C T I O N S :
- Overview of VPIC
- Getting started

The project manager's serenity prayer:
Grant me the serenity to prioritize the things I
  cannot delegate,
the courage to say no when I need to,
and the wisdom to know when to go home.

VINCE FAYAD WALKED INTO THE meeting room with several sheets of easel paper taped together and proceeded to cover the front wall with the huge blank sheet. He introduced a brainstorming process and, within minutes, had the group of engineers calling out ideas and suggestions in a freewheeling brainstorming session that quickly generated 256 possible product improvements.

Vince, a trainer with a large equipment manufacturer in Portland, Oregon, has become an expert at the *process* of project management. Without an engineering background or any in-depth understanding of the product being discussed, he was able to help the engineering group take the first steps in project management: identifying possibilities and creating a vision. Later the group sorted the ideas, weeding out the weak ones and selecting the best. These were then refined into well-defined improvement projects with specific and measurable expected results. By their second session, the group had developed a project vision that was ready to be implemented.

Becoming an expert at managing projects may seem difficult simply because every project is unique. By definition, projects are nonroutine. Each has a limited and distinct set of resources, its own specific goals, a unique mix of people involved, a particular time line, and distinctive environments. Because every project is unique, every time we start a new project, we may feel as if we're reinventing the wheel. How can we master something that changes every time we do it?

What Vince Fayad dramatically demonstrated is that we can become experts at a *process*—something that happens repetitively in a predetermined manner. While each project is different, all projects can be managed by using a well-defined, repeatable process. We become expert project managers by applying that process which guides us through the necessary steps of visualization, planning, implementation, and closure. This simple project management model can be applied to any project—simple or complex, technical or personal, long-range or short.

Effective project management is a *repeatable* process.

Because the process is consistent and can be applied to all projects, anyone can become adept at successfully completing projects. Regardless of the project, the project management *process* remains the same. You plug the process in and it guides you to successful project completion. While complex projects often incorporate all the tools that come with the process, simpler projects generally use only a few. The tools are flexible, but the process doesn't change.

In our increasingly demanding world, the people who succeed will be the ones who can initiate and complete challenging projects. They will be the ones who know how to create a vision that engages everyone involved in the project. They will be able to define expected results; delegate responsibility; break the project down into manageable chunks; develop achievable schedules; communicate concisely, clearly, and rapidly; adjust quickly to changes; monitor progress; and accept nothing short of project success.

VPIC: A SIMPLE MODEL FOR PROJECT SUCCESS

The following is a summary of the four-step model that makes project management easy. Each step will be explained in detail in the following chapters. The four steps are these: visualize, plan, implement, and close.

Visualize

What is the project supposed to look like when we're done, and *why* are we doing it? Projects begin with a dream or an idea, and the first step in project management is to create a clear picture of what the end result will look like. What are we trying to accomplish? What's the definition of the project? Are we clear about our objective, or is it still vague?

Most of us have worked on a project where we had one end result in mind and someone else had a totally different vision of the objective. The visualization step helps us make sure the vision is clear, that everyone involved knows what the objective is and what it will look like when it's done.

Typically when people begin a project, they jump into planning or even implementation before they have a clear idea of what they're planning or implementing. There is a difference between doing things right and doing the right thing. Once we have a clear vision of where we're going and what we want to achieve, we're ready for the next stage—planning.

Plan

This stage determines *how* we will achieve the objective (what tasks need to be done), *who* will do which tasks, *when* and *where* they will do them, and *how much* the project will cost. The planning process takes the overall objective and breaks it down into manageable pieces. Even huge, overwhelming projects start to look doable when they are broken down into bite-size chunks and individual tasks. The people involved with the project gain confidence and commitment as they begin to feel that the project can be successfully completed. This simplifies the next stage—implementation.

Implement

This is where the dream becomes the reality. Implementation involves the communication, coordination, monitoring, and controlling needed to keep a project on track toward successful completion. It also includes adjusting for the inevitable changes that occur. This stage depends heavily on the day planner as the tool for making sure all tasks and details are in alignment and on schedule. When the objectives of the project are reached, it's time for the next stage—closure.

Close

By definition, all projects have a specific objective, and when that objective is reached, the project is finished. This stage of project management is a time to tie up loose ends, compare the outcome of the project with the intended results, and celebrate, honor, and reward the efforts of everyone involved. This is an important learning opportunity that can provide critical lessons for improving our project completion skills. It can also strengthen relationships for future project efforts.

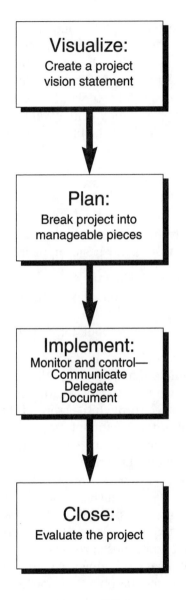

FIGURE III-1
Project Management Process

Becoming a project completion expert is increasingly critical for each of us. The simple four-step model outlined above
gives you a process that can be successfully applied to any
project. In the following chapters, we will introduce you to
many project management tools. The tools you use may
change with each project, or you may want to customize them
to a particular situation, but the project management *process*
will always be the same.

GETTING STARTED

Before we actually dive into the details of this simple four-step
VPIC model, you need a few basic supplies:

- A day planner (see Chapter 4)
- Tabbed dividers for your day planner to serve as your
  project tabs
- A separate project notebook for completed projects

Each time you begin a significant project—meaning one
that is not so simple that you can outline the steps directly
into your day planner—you will create a project tab in your
day planner. As we go through the steps of the VPIC process,
you will keep all of the documentation and notes about the
project behind this project tab. This will keep all the important information about this project at your fingertips.

You will also keep a separate notebook for completed projects. Once the project is finished, you will transfer all of the
documentation and notes to this notebook. Some projects
may become so large or complex that they require separate
notebooks and files. For these projects, you will keep only the
current information and schedules in your day planner. Older,
more complex documentation will be kept in the project notebook or files.

Now that we have a basic guideline to follow, we are ready
to start the first step of the *process* of project management:
visualize.

CHAPTER 6

VISUALIZE
The First Step Toward Success

COMING ATTRACTIONS:
- Begin at the end
- The big picture question
- Success defined
- SMART vision statements
- Dealing with the number one excuse

Vision without action is merely a dream.
Action without vision just passes the time.
Vision with action can change the world.

—JOEL BARKER

THREE TALES: ONE FICTION AND TWO TRUE

Tale Number One

Many long years ago, the only child of Mr. and Mrs. Crusoe sailed across the sea to find fame and fortune in a strange land. Rob was a hardy and adventurous lad, and when disaster struck his hapless ship, he managed to find his way to a deserted but pleasant island.

Rather than bewail his fate, he immediately jumped into action and decided to build a canoe from one of the large palm trees that surrounded him. Using an ax he had salvaged from the ship, Rob spent days felling the tree and weeks hollowing it out. Finally his canoe was ready, and Rob could escape from his watery prison.

He tugged on the canoe. . . . Nothing. He pushed, he pulled, he shoved with all his might, but the canoe would not move. Only a hundred yards of beach lay between Rob's canoe and the beckoning sea, but that distance proved to be an impossible barrier.

Rob, you see, had a perfectly good vision—of how to build a canoe. What he lacked was a vision of how to get off the island, which would have included the canoe *and* a way to get the canoe into the water.

Tale Number Two

In a recent time and place, Gordon and his wife finished building their dream home, a lovely brick house with large white pillars located in a rural area. Near the house was a pond with geese. After they moved in, Gordon's mother came to visit and brought some of his childhood possessions. Included in one of the boxes was a picture Gordon had drawn as a child—of a house with white pillars and a pond with geese on it!

While Gordon didn't remember creating the picture from his childhood, it's obvious that he created a powerful vision which he turned into a reality many years later.

Tale Number Three

I recently had an experience similar to Gordon's when my son and I were looking for a house. We had looked at everything on the market and had given up and decided to build our own. I discovered a design software program and began laying out a floor plan that had our major requirements in it—a connected kitchen and family room for me, a large separate living area with space for a pool table for Seth, and so on. We had a great time designing our home, and several weeks later we had it just about the way we wanted it. Then my mom called and said there was a new listing in the newspaper that looked interesting. Seth and I went to see the house right away and were amazed—it was our house! It was almost exactly the floor plan we had designed. We were so excited that we made an immediate offer, and suddenly the house was ours.

Everything—a house, a deserted island escape, a moon landing, a career, a symphony, and tonight's dinner—everything begins with a vision, a thought, a dream, an idea. The first step in creating reality is seeing the end result we want. Skipping this step is starting the car, pointing it in a direction, and hoping we'll wind up somewhere. We will, absolutely, wind up somewhere, but, without a clear understanding of where we want to go and a road map to help us get there, who knows where it will be? Like poor Rob on his deserted island, we may wind up with a canoe but no water. Perhaps Alice and the Cheshire Cat say it best:

> "Would you tell me, please, which way I ought to walk from here?" asked Alice.
> "That depends a good deal on where you want to get to," said the cat.
> "I don't much care where," said Alice.
> "Then it doesn't much matter which way you walk," said the cat.

We call this the Alice in Wonderland approach to project management, when we jump right into projects with a vague idea and then wander aimlessly around doing things here and there until the project fails or is forgotten. Since most of us do care where we get to, there must be a better way . . . and there is; it's called having a vision of where we want to go.

FIGURE 6-1
Alice

BEGIN AT THE END

At the beginning of any project, there is a familiar set of obstacles and barriers: limited resources or time and an abundance of sacred cows and political agendas, which create hidden land mines. If you look at most projects from the front, where all the problems sit, they often appear overwhelmingly difficult and time-consuming. There is a way around this lamentable view: begin at the end. Look at the desired end result. This is sometimes called "working backward from perfect," "future vision," or "wouldn't it be nice if . . . ?"

The power of looking at the future is that it skips over all the hazardous territory in between you and your goal. It lets you ignore all the differences in methods, technologies, and ideologies and focus instead on the desired outcome. Once people agree about where they want to go, they can often compromise on methods and create new possibilities. Focusing on the outcome develops a shared vision that creates energy, enthusiasm, optimism, and high commitment, and this outlook makes people willing to find a compromise on methodologies.

A powerful vision generates enthusiasm and commitment.

Another benefit of a vision statement is the reduction of fear. Fear blocks the successful completion of many projects and is an obstacle to even beginning others. If we see only the problems and obstacles that come with a project, it's easy to avoid the commitment necessary to take it on. A clear vision stimulates our passion and gives us the courage to attempt the project and to keep struggling against obstacles until the project is successfully completed.

Few projects, however, involve only one person's vision. We face an additional challenge when we enter into a situation where someone else's vision is now ours to implement, as in an assignment from a boss or a teacher. Or we may be part of a team responsible for the manifestation of a particular vision. The vision did not originate solely in our own mind. We have to find a way to create a shared vision to define success for the project.

THE BIG PICTURE QUESTION

One way to clarify a vision is to ask the big picture question. This question focuses on the desired outcome rather than on possible methods of getting there. Here's the format of the big picture question: _____ , (boss, customer, client, stake-holder) when you think about _____ (description of the project) what's most important to you?

Example: Your boss has asked you to plan this year's strategic planning meeting. There are a lot of variables involved: where to hold the meeting (first-class or economy), when to hold the meeting, whether to have a highly structured program or leave a lot of open time, whether or not to have a facilitator, and so on. So, you ask: "Boss, when you think about this strategic planning meeting, what's most important to you?"

This open-ended question leaves a lot of room for discussion of objectives and goals and helps everyone involved with the project clarify the vision.

Asking the big picture question clarifies expectations.

DEFINING SUCCESS

One of the primary reasons for spending the time to develop a shared vision is to clarify the definition of success. Without this step, every person involved with the project is likely to have different success criteria. The financial person might have return-on-investment ideas while the marketing person has market-share criteria; the manufacturing person might have production goals in mind, and of course the customer may be looking for something that will solve a specific problem and will not cost too much.

As a brief exercise in my project management seminars, I ask participants why projects fail. The answers generally fall into the following categories:

- Unclear goals or objectives
- Changing scope (scope creep)
- Not enough resources

- Conflicting priorities
- Lack of knowledge or technical expertise
- Poor communications
- Lack of leadership
- Lack of management support
- Lack of teamwork and commitment
- Poor (or no) planning
- Changing or losing key team members
- Political issues

There is a wide variety of reasons for project failure, but there seems to be one generally agreed-on definition of failure: the project did not meet expectations. Regardless of the reasons, if a project did not meet the specific expectations of those involved, then it is a failure. This makes defining success relatively easy.

Success equals met expectations.

By definition, then, success depends on developing a thorough understanding of expectations. However, it is critical to determine *whose* expectations determine success—those of the team, the boss, the client or customer, or the shareholder. The answer to this question identifies the project stakeholders, and until we know who the stakeholders are, we cannot possibly determine the expectations that need to be met to create a successful project.

Think about this situation: Two party planners agree on a project: *Let's have a feast!* On the next page, there is a view of their mental visions.

What do you think will happen as they try to implement their vision? Chaos, hurt feelings, snafus, blaming, and ultimate failure are only some of the possibilities unless the planners develop a shared vision and a statement of their shared expectations.

FIGURE 6-2
"Let's Have a Feast"

⌘ **Ponder Point:** *Think about a current project and
list the expectations of each of the stakeholders.*

VISION STATEMENT

Obviously it's important to explore the mental visions of the
key members of the project team. An excellent way to do this
is to create a group mindmap capturing the ideas of everyone
in the group. The two primary questions to ask during this
discussion are:

1. What does the completed project look like?
2. Who and what defines success?

Here is a hypothetical situation:

You and your family decide to build a backyard pool. You're sitting around the kitchen table mindmapping the project, and you've asked the others for their input by saying, "As you think about having a swimming pool, what kinds of things are important to you?"

SARAH, 16: "It's important to me to have all my friends over for pool parties."

DAD: "It's important for me that it doesn't have to be cleaned all the time."

MOM: "I would like it if it were long enough to swim laps."

GARY, 12: "I want a diving board!"

EVERYONE: It's important to have it by summer.

From this mindmap, you can write a vision statement containing the following two elements:

Two Elements of a Vision Statement _____

- **Project definition**—a simple, clear statement of the project description (shared vision) stated in terms of what, when, and where.
- **Project expected results**—a concise, detailed list of what the project needs to accomplish.

Project Definition for Swimming Pool Example _____

Build a high-quality, lap-diving-swimming pool surrounded by a party area with a barbecue by May 1.

Project expected results _____

1. Build a quality swimming pool 50 feet long with deep end and diving board.
2. Surround area with attractive brick party area with barbecue pit.

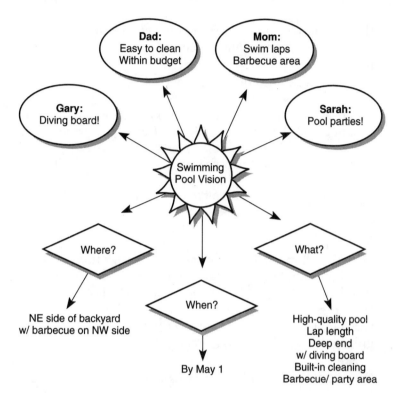

FIGURE 6-3
Mindmap of Swimming Pool Project

3. Costs not to exceed $25,000.
4. Include self-cleaning system and pool cover.

The order of the expected results is important. In the above example, listing quality, the attributes of the pool, and its environment in the first two expected results presumes that these expectations are more important than the budget limitation and ease of cleaning. Not that these aren't critical expectations, but if a trade-off is required, the priority is already established.

One of the most notable projects in recent history was the space program. In 1961 President John F. Kennedy defined the project when he called for landing a man on the moon and returning him safely by the end of the decade. When NASA began working on the program, there were three primary expected results:

1. Enhance the prestige and image of the United States.
2. Ensure the safety of the crew.
3. Gather scientific data.

At first glance, these expected results appear to be in the wrong order. Surely safety of the crew would be the first priority. However, if you think about it, if safety had been the first priority, the space program would never have happened. The only way to guarantee absolute safety would have been to keep the crew on terra firma. The *first* priority was the enhancement of the prestige and image of the United States— remember this was after we had been humiliated by Sputnik. Otherwise there would have been no need for the space program.

Before we go on to the planning stage, we must have both the project definition and the statement of expected results. Many times, however, projects are tossed onto our desk without this information. For example, your boss might hand you an assignment to develop a same-day product delivery system. In this example, you are given an expected result without knowing what the project is that will accomplish it. The project might involve a new computer-order entry system, a new computerized warehouse system, additional staff, or a project to regionalize the distribution centers. These possibilities need to be explored, which is sometimes a project in and of itself, before a project definition and expected results statement can be written to meet the expectations of the boss.

A clear definition and a clear list of expected results are critical to project success.

Here's another example: You're assigned responsibility for the company's annual charity fund-raising picnic, and you're given this project definition: "A charity fund-raising picnic is to be held on June 17 to raise $10,000."

That's a simple, clear statement of the project, but we still haven't clarified all the possible stakeholders and expected results. The project becomes more challenging when we discover (by asking the stakeholders what is important) the following expectations:

- The charity involved not only needs the money but also wants to raise community awareness.
- Management wants to make sure that 50 percent of all employees attend and that employee donations average $20.
- Employees want an event that's fun for the families, especially children.
- Local media will cover the event if it's unique, colorful, and involves local celebrities.
- The money raised will provide food and clothing at the local shelter.

By looking only at the definition or only at the expected results, we do not have the complete picture. When either piece of the vision statement is missing, we need to work with the stakeholders to further clarify the vision. This sounds pretty simple, but I've found that it's extremely difficult to keep people focused on the vision. They keep wanting to jump immediately into the detailed planning stage.

I encourage groups to use a brainstorming process with one team member as the mindmapping facilitator. Everyone in the team tosses out ideas, which are then mindmapped. Start with three branches on the map: What, When, Where. When all three of these questions are answered, the project definition

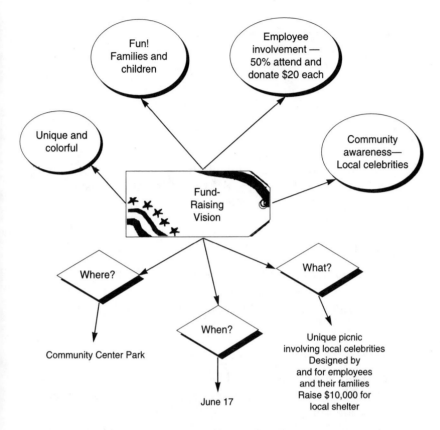

FIGURE 6-4
Mindmap of Fund-Raising Project

is complete. Expected results can be clarified and prioritized on the mindmap. This may take a few rough drafts to complete. Eventually, the team goes from the creative part of the process to the editing part, getting clearer and clearer about the project.

This is not a lengthy process. Most groups can mindmap expectations and develop a project definition in ten to fifteen minutes. For an extremely complex problem you may have to do a preliminary study-project to evaluate possibilities before you begin the actual solution project. Once the mapping is done, the definition can be written at the top of a project task map form (see Figure 6-5), which will be discussed in more detail in the next chapter.

SMART VISION STATEMENTS

When the rough draft of a definition and expected results are completed, see if they're SMART (Specific, Measurable, Achievable, Relevant and Time-dimensioned).

Specific

This is a reminder to be clear and specific in the wording we use in our vision statement—"five-course banquet," for example, as opposed to something vague like "feast."

Measurable

Our vision statement should be as measurable as possible (and feasible). An objective of "raising money" is much less measurable than "raising $10,000." The second is easy to evaluate and determine success at the end of the project; the first is not.

Achievable

Use achievability as an up-front reality check. Is this project really doable given the available time, talent, and resources? Is the project realistic and achievable enough to pursue any further? Be careful, however, not to let this pull you into detailed planning and trying to solve the problems. Detailed planning may eventually be necessary to determine the potential for success of the project, but at this stage you just want to eliminate the obviously improbable projects. Some (perhaps many) projects can be eliminated right here with a

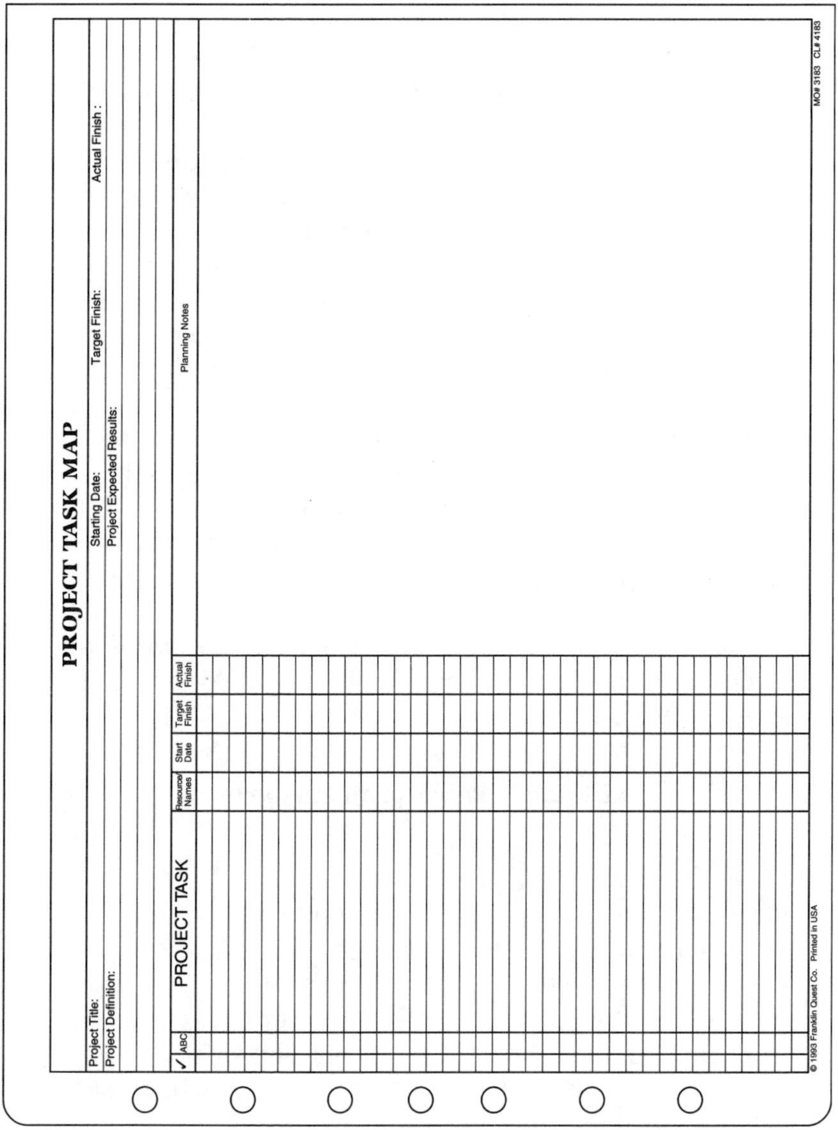

FIGURE 6-5
Example: Task Map Form

cursory but realistic look at what will be necessary for success.

I once received a letter from a woman who attended my class in Washington, D.C. Her letter began, "Thanks to you, I did not finish the project I was working on in your class. In fact, thanks to you, I never even started it." She went on to explain that while working on the project in class, she realized that there was much more involved in this project than she had first imagined, and it was clear to her that now was not the right time in her life to undertake such a project.

As disappointing as this outcome may be, it's better to realize a project's futility at this stage than during the implementation stage. If a project needs to be killed, that should be done as soon as possible, either during the visualization stage or the planning stage. Projects that are begun (implemented) are open pits that swallow resources, and only the ones that are successfully completed are worth the resources poured into them. Projects should either die early . . . or succeed.

Kill unworkable projects early.

Relevant

Relevance is perhaps the most important criterion. Pause for a moment and look at the project in connection with your values. Ask yourself, Do I have a value that supports this project? Then ask, Is it relevant at this time? Does the project make sense in the context of everything else we're doing?

This, too, is a place where many projects should be stopped before they go any further.

Time-Dimensioned

One characteristic that makes a project unique is that it is temporary rather than ongoing. If projects do not have a deadline, they don't qualify as projects; they're just "round toits"—those things you can do when you "get around to it." If the project is to be a priority, it needs a target deadline. We may not be able to finalize the deadline until we are through more of the planning stage, but we should be able to set a rough target date of when we would like to see the project completed.

CHECK YOUR VISION STATEMENT. ARE THE EXPECTED RESULTS . . .

- Specific?
- Measurable?
- Achievable?
- Relevant?
- Time-dimensioned?

Checking our vision statement with these five criteria assures us that we have a guideline for the remainder of the project. Also, the process of creating this shared vision establishes a team that is committed to the implementation of the project. The vision statement makes the planning, the implementation, and the closing stages all much easier to manage.

DEALING WITH THE NUMBER ONE EXCUSE: NO TIME

Defining the project and expected results seems like an obvious first step, yet most people I talk to in my seminars state that they rarely do it. When I ask why, they say they don't have time. This excuse does not consider the enormous payback of visualizing the expected results, which accomplishes the following:

- Determines where we're going (and where we're *not* going)

- Clarifies our priorities about what's most important in the project
- Generates energy and commitment by aligning our values and our projects

The process we've described generally only takes fifteen to thirty minutes. How could we justify skipping this critical step?

Which takes more time: stopping to buy a map or getting lost?

Imagine walking into your local automobile club office and asking for a map. "A map to where?" the clerk asks. "I don't know," you respond. "Maybe some place warm, maybe with a beach or a lake . . . Oh, just give me a map." The clerk would probably think you were crazy and tell you that as soon as you choose your destination, she will give you a map.

Sound bizarre? It's not all that different from the way we approach our projects every day.

My friend Jerry tells a story about his family's move to the Midwest, a move dictated by his company. After a bitter, record-breaking winter, it was clear that Jerry's wife was not happy in the new location. During one deep breakfast conversation, she finally explained all the things she did not like about the city. Jerry asked, "Where would you rather live?" She paused for a moment and replied, "Not here!"

Jerry said to me, "Lynne, this is how a lot of projects begin. There is an expected result ('not here') but no clear vision."

For Jerry and his wife, a lot of clarification work was needed to move from the vague "not here" concept to a clear idea of where an acceptable "here" would be. Finally, after going through this clarification process, a job offer in Atlanta came up, and both of them agreed that Atlanta met their expectations.

Once expectations are clear, a vision statement can be plugged into a project task map form (see Figure 6-6) that will help as a planning and tracking tool. This form is designed to help the entire process of brainstorming, detailing, and implementing tasks. It will be discussed in detail in the next chapter.

The visualize stage may take a few moments, or you may need days, weeks, months, or, yes, even years to completely clarify your values, expectations, and objectives. The point is that this stage—the vision—must be clear before you are ready to begin the planning process.

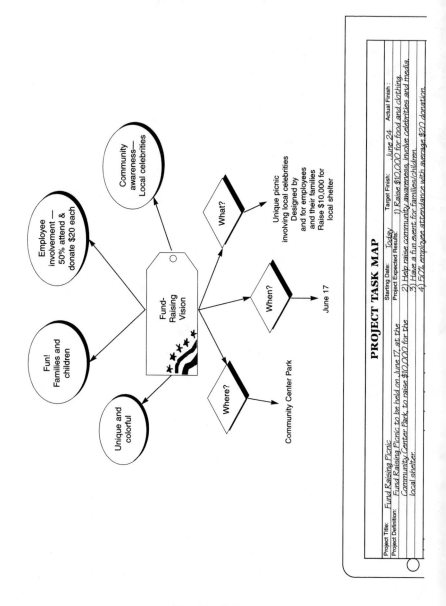

FIGURE 6-6
Clarifying the Vision Statement in a Task Map Form

CHAPTER 7

PLAN

Outguessing and Outsmarting Failure

COMING ATTRACTIONS:
- Breaking project resistance
- The seven-step planning model
- Question-storming

Take charge of your life! To act intelligently and effectively, we still must have a plan. To the proverb which says, "a journey of a thousand miles begins with a single step," I would add the words "and a road map."

—CECILE M. SPRINGER

We've determined *where* we want to go . . . Vision Statement; and *why* we want to go there . . . Governing Values; it's now time to determine *how* to get there . . . a Plan.

Most of us work on more than one project at a time, so we have a lot of conflicting and competing demands on our time and resources. The planning process gives us a blueprint for managing these demands and successfully completing our projects. Crawford Greenwaldt, a former president of Du Pont, said that "for every moment spent planning, you can save three or four moments of execution time."

The payoff for careful planning is the difference between success and failure; it's the way we outguess and outsmart failure.

BREAKING PROJECT RESISTANCE

Most of us have experienced project resistance, that dark cloud that hangs over us when a lengthy, pressing project needs our attention. We think about it, fret about it, chew our fingernails, but never quite get to it. The cloud gets bigger and darker, and we start to wake up at night in a cold sweat. Because the project is getting bigger in our minds, we start to think we need more and more time for it. "I'll get started as soon as I have a free hour" turns into "I need a minimum of a half day to really get into it." Pretty soon the project seems so big and evil that there's no way we have enough time to do it justice so we keep putting it off, and the guilt grows.

Project resistance comes from fear.

The following model provides a process that reduces project-related stress by giving you a way to systematically look at the project and break it down into manageable chunks.

PROJECT PLANNING AT A GLANCE: A SEVEN-STEP MODEL

Here are the seven steps of project management, which we will discuss in detail in the rest of this chapter:

PROJECT PLANNING IN SEVEN STEPS _____

1. **Constraints**—prioritizing the three factors that define performance in all projects
2. **Hot spots**—identifying possible hot spots
3. **Hunks, chunks, and bites**—breaking the project down into manageable pieces
4. **Forms**—entering sequenced tasks on project management forms, which help guide the process
5. **Who**—clarifying who is responsible for each part of the project
6. **When**—prioritizing and scheduling each piece and task
7. **Cost**—determining the project budget

STEP 1. PRIORITIZE PROJECT CONSTRAINTS

The first things to look at on a project are the limiting factors. There are always three constraints involved with any project: quality, schedule, and resources—sometimes referred to as good, fast, and cheap. While the stakeholders in a project will always want all three, it seldom happens that way. If you want high quality immediately, you will need resources. If you have to have the lowest priced product and you have to have it today, you probably won't get the highest quality. And excellent low-priced products generally take time to design, develop, and produce. So it's important to know, realistically, what the trade-offs are for this project.

Universal constraints: quality, schedule, resources

Our job as project managers is to maintain the best balance and harmony among these three constraints. But when hard decisions are required, we have to know which of the three constraints will have top priority. The only way to find out is to ask questions.

Assume for a moment that your boss gives you a new project. You ask her, "Which is most important—quality, schedule, or resources?" She says (naturally), "All three."

There is one way you might handle this all-too-typical situation and discover what the real priorities are:

"Boss, I know it's important for this project to be high quality and to come in on time and within budget, but how would you like me to handle difficulties that might come up during the project?

"What if something goes wrong and threatens to delay the project? Would you want to add more resources—people, equipment, and supplies—to make sure we meet the deadline, or is the deadline more flexible than the budget? Would you consider changing the scope or technical specifications (quality) if it looked like we couldn't meet them during the prescribed time frame with our existing budgeted resources?"

Understanding constraint priorities makes decisions easier.

By asking the right questions, you will begin to understand how the constraints are prioritized and what to do when situations begin to change on the project . . . as they always do. While quality, schedule, and resources are always important, the reality is they have different weights that affect the management of our projects.

I once prepared a train-the-trainer program that *had* to be delivered in six weeks. If something had gone wrong, we would have had to apply more resources to the project, or reduce its scope, because our deadline was absolutely inflexible.

Some product contracts do contain inflexible technical specifications. If there are problems meeting those requirements, the organization has to decide whether to sacrifice the budget or the delivery date, or both. Other projects are more constrained by budget requirements, and problems require a trade-off between quality and deadline.

Question-Storming

Tom Wujec in his book, *Five Star Mind,* tells a story about Rembrandt's famous painting *The Night Watch,* which dramatically illustrates the importance of questioning.

> When it [the painting] was restored and returned to Amsterdam's Rijksmuseum, the curators performed a simple yet remarkable experiment. They asked visitors to submit questions about the painting. The curators then prepared answers to over fifty questions according to popularity.
>
> Some of these questions focused on issues which curators usually don't like to include: How much does the painting cost? Has this painting ever been forged? Are there mistakes in the painting? Other questions focused on traditional artistic issues: Why did Rembrandt paint the subject? Who were the people in the painting? What techniques did Rembrandt pioneer in this particular work?
>
> In a room next to the gallery which held the painting, the curators papered the walls with these questions (and answers). Visitors had to pass through this room before entering the gallery.
>
> The curious outcome was that the average length of time people spent viewing the painting increased from six minutes to over half an hour. Visitors alternated between reading questions and answers and examining the painting. They said that the questions encouraged them to look longer, to look closer, and to remember more. The questions helped them create richer ideas about the painting and to see the painting in new ways. *Like a series of magnets, the questions attracted the visitors' thoughts to fresh ideas* [emphasis added].

Projects are almost always a learning experience: cutting through old patterns to do things in new ways, putting together data to find solutions to problems, and finding more effective ways to use resources. According to Wujec, asking questions puts us in a "ready-to-learn frame of mind by stimulating curiosity." Therefore, one way to create a learning mind-set for a project is to ask questions.

Try having a question-storming session. Have your team members write questions they'd like to have answered about the project on separate sticky notes. Spend about ten minutes letting them write down all the questions they can think of. Then have them read their questions aloud and put them on a large sheet of easel paper. The questions can then be grouped into the four categories of information:

- Things we know and know we know
- Things we know but don't know we know
- Things we don't know and know we don't know
- Things we don't know and don't know we don't know

The danger, of course, comes from the things we don't know and don't know we don't know. In the space program, these were called the "deadly unk-unks"—the unknown unknowns. Question-storming can help identify the unk-unks by deliberately exploring all the things we don't know. It can also reveal potential hot spots.

Beware the frumious unk-unks.

STEP 2: EVALUATE POTENTIAL HOT SPOTS

A sense of euphoria often accompanies a new project. We've all caught the vision, excitement is in the air, enthusiasm is high, and the entire team is ready to charge. One of the hardest things to do at this point is to stop and think about possible problems and potential hot spots. When we see visions of grandeur and success in front of us, the last thing we want to do is think about all the things that could go wrong.

In Joyce's book *Transformation Thinking,* she calls this the "Cross Your Fingers" thinking pitfall. We cross our fingers and hope that something will work rather than thinking through all the possible ramifications if it doesn't and creating backup plans. Contingency planning isn't an idle activity for organizations with time to spare; it's a way of thinking. It reflects a realistic understanding that no matter how certain we think we are, we can never know *everything* about anything, and we can never predict with certainty what tomorrow will bring. In other words, we could be wrong. And if we can be wrong, then looking for possible hot spots and making backup plans isn't just a nice idea; it's a fundamental part of the process.

Years ago over-the-counter drug manufacturers did not identify packaging as a potential hot spot. When people died from some Tylenol capsules laced with cyanide, however, this became an immediate issue and tamper-proof packaging became mandatory. We will probably never be able to identify all the potential hot spots, but in the process of looking for them we can identify bumps in the road that can be eliminated before they become potholes that can sink our projects.

One of the best ways to build this activity into the process is to hold an official "hot spot identification" brainstorming session at the beginning of every project. Formal hot spot meetings will let everyone on the team know what to look out for and will help them work to avoid these potential trouble areas. Gather the team together and create a mindmap of all the potential problems and unwanted possibilities.

Put a circle in the middle of a flip chart or a whiteboard with the term "hot spots" in the center. Gather around the flip chart, give each person a colored pen, and start brainstorming. Since all team members will be writing their own ideas, it's important for them to say the idea aloud so everyone else can hear it and it can help trigger more ideas. Even if the group has not been trained to do mindmapping, this is such a simple technique that they will catch on quickly.

A group that stands up with all members recording their own ideas will generate more energy and ideas than a group that is seated with one person recording the ideas. If you have a large group, however, you may need to use a facilitator-recorder. That person should be trained in ways to stimulate group thinking and energy.

Energy Tips

A great deal of the effectiveness of brainstorming sessions depends on managing the group's energy. Here are a few energy management tips:

- Have everyone stand up.
- Give everyone a pen so they can write their own ideas. Have people say the ideas out loud as they write them. This gives everyone else a chance to see and hear all of the ideas.
- Use large sheets of paper. Cover a whole wall.
- Change marker or pen colors.
- Have people change positions around the paper.
- Draw empty lines off the center focus. The brain will start to fill in the lines.

Once the group has identified as many potential hot spots and hazards as possible, continue the brainstorming and mindmapping process to explore alternative solutions for some of the major hot spots.

Another reason for having the hot spot meeting is that it allows all team members to voice any reservations they might have. Often, at the end of a project, especially if it has failed, one or more members of the group will say, "I knew this would never work, because . . ." The hot spot meeting gets these thoughts out in the open at the beginning and gives the group a chance to resolve them. This helps improve group commitment as each person has had a chance to voice his or her reservations and have them either satisfactorily explained away or validated as a potential problem that needs to be addressed.

Hot spot meetings identify potential trouble spots and build group commitment.

Also, remember that a project should either die early or succeed. Hot spot meetings can identify ways to avoid obstacles and barriers. Occasionally, however, they may reveal an insurmountable barrier that makes the project a no-go. Better to find that out now than later after we've entered the implementation stage and begun pouring resources into the project.

Most potential hot spots can be dealt with, however, if they're identified in advance—another example of how planning helps us outguess and outsmart failure.

TIP—Keep all hot-spot meeting flip chart pages for later reference. It may be weeks or months later that one of these hot spots occurs, but you'll be glad to have the notes to help deal with a particular challenge.

STEP 3: BREAK THE PROJECT DOWN INTO HUNKS, CHUNKS, AND BITES

The oldest project management joke asks, "How do you eat an elephant?" The answer: "One bite at a time." While this joke is probably no longer politically correct, it captures the essence of project planning—breaking the project down into manageable chunks. This eliminates stress and generates energy as we begin to see, realistically, how we are going to accomplish our vision.

We will again use the mindmapping tool as a way to start breaking down the project. We start with the big picture and then break the project down into smaller levels of detail, as far as necessary to identify clear personal accountability (who is doing what?). In order to apply this technique to simple projects (we will cover more complex projects later) you will need the following:

- Paper or whiteboard for rough drafts of your mindmaps. You may map out several ideas and alternatives before you settle on the approach you think will work best. Later, the final draft will go onto a project form. Use the largest

paper you can find—flip charts, large computer pages, sheets of butcher paper, or ledger copier paper. If you use 8½-by-11-inch paper, turn it sideways; it helps break mental ruts. The advantage of letter-size paper is that it fits well in a project file folder for later reference.
- Colored markers. Indulge yourself with good markers in a variety of colors. Color can be used to show organization, to stimulate energy, or just because it's fun.
- Project task map form. This form can easily be created with a spread sheet program or, if you prefer, a prepared form is available from Franklin Quest (see Appendix A).

Henry Ford said, "Nothing is particularly hard if you divide it into small jobs." And in simplistic terms, project planning is not much more than dividing the project down into manageable pieces, deciding who's going to do what, when and where each task will be done, and how much it will cost. The first step is to identify the major pieces of the project—the hunks.

Hunks (Major Pieces)

Hunks are the major subdivisions, or pieces, of the project. If you were going to remodel your house, you might break the project down into the following hunks:

- Budget
- Design
- Construction
- Decorating

By identifying the major pieces of the project, we begin to make them clear and manageable, especially in terms of accountability. This process gives us a clear overview of the work that needs to be done. Some major pieces, such as budget, are standard on most projects. Sometimes the budget can be clarified at the beginning of the project, especially when a budget limit is part of the initial project assignment.

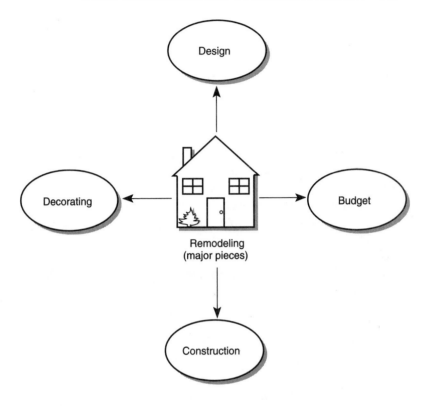

FIGURE 7-1
Mindmap of Remodel Project (Major Pieces)

More often, however, the full budget cannot be developed until later, when more detailed information and specific tasks are determined. We will look at the budget in more detail later.

Major pieces should encompass all the work to be done on a project. If you can think of any task, no matter how small, that does not fit under one of the major pieces, you have not yet determined all of the major pieces. Another example of looking at the major pieces occurred when I was developing Franklin's project management train-the-trainers workshop. My first step was to break the project down into four major pieces:

- Leader's guide
- Workshop video
- Training kit
- Materials

Chunks (Minor Pieces)

Most project hunks can be further divided into smaller pieces, or chunks. This process—breaking the project down into smaller and smaller pieces until we reach the level of individual tasks which can be assigned and scheduled—makes the project clear and manageable, especially in terms of accountability.

In the train-the-trainer program, for example, two of the major pieces needed to be broken down further. "Leader's guide" was broken down into three chunks, or minor pieces:

- Writing
- Artwork
- Production

"Materials" was broken down into two smaller, more manageable pieces:

- Materials to order, including books and other supplies
- Materials to ship, to get all the program materials to the training site

Bites

Once a project is broken down into major and minor pieces, the necessary tasks—the bites—begin to be apparent. A task is a bite-size activity that can generally be done in a short time by one person. It's what you might find on your daily task list in your day planner—something small and manageable that does not need to be broken down any further and that can be checked off or arrowed forward at the end of the day.

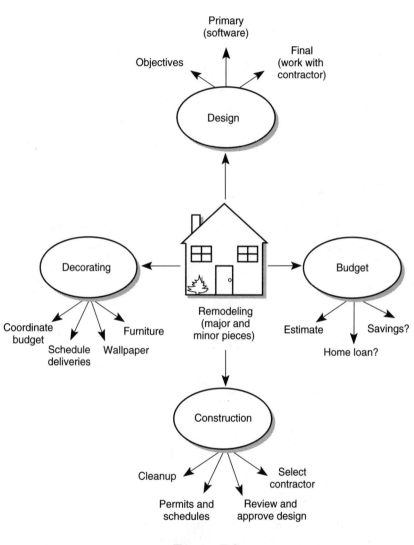

FIGURE 7-2
Mindmap of Remodeling Project
(Major and Minor Pieces)

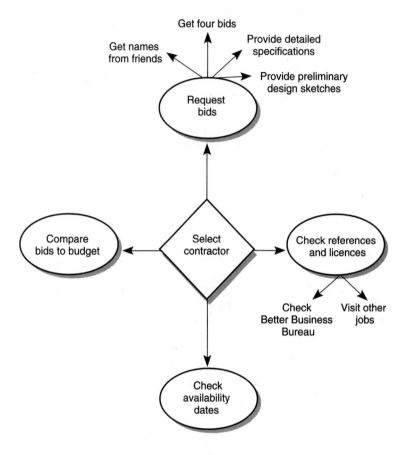

FIGURE 7-3
Task Mindmap

Take into consideration some personal preferences and style differences when deciding how far down to break the detail of a major or minor piece. Different people are comfortable with different levels of detail. I might be comfortable with a task that stated "Edit leader's guide," while someone else might want more detail, such as: "Edit chapter one of leader's guide." Since tasks are assigned to individuals, it's up to that person to describe the tasks most effectively.

TIP—Tasks are the action steps of a project . . . use verbs. Each task should be an action that can be checked off when completed. When all of the tasks related to a minor or major piece are completed, that hunk or chunk is done.

In our train-the-trainer example, we immediately broke the training video down into tasks instead of dividing it into any intermediate minor pieces. Here is the task list:

Meet with producer; develop concept
Write script and storyboard
Shoot video
Edit video
Produce five copies

A task breakdown of one chunk of the remodeling project might look like this:

WALLPAPERING _____

Select and order paper
Purchase materials (detailed on "purchases" tasks list)
Remove old paper
Prepare walls
Hang new paper

STEP 4: ENTER SEQUENCED TASKS ON PLANNING FORMS

Once we understand what needs to be done, we should look at the logical sequence of the tasks—which hunks, chunks, and bites need to be done in what order. Sequencing of tasks is critical, since certain tasks may have to be completed before the next ones can be started. Regarding sequencing, there are two primary types of tasks:

- Parallel—a task that can be done during the same time frame as one or more other tasks.
- Dependent—a task that cannot begin until certain predecessor tasks are complete.

Where tasks are independent of each other, sequencing is not as important and tasks can be done concurrently. A primary purpose of sequencing is to determine the *predecessor and dependent* tasks, because any slippage in the performance of those tasks can adversely affect a series of other tasks and, ultimately, the entire project.

To get a general overview of timing, determine the sequence of the major pieces. Again, do this knowing that there are pieces and tasks that are dependent on other tasks, as well as parallel tasks that can be done at the same time. While all the major project pieces may be independent of each other, it is more likely that there is an interdependence which makes careful sequencing important. Next, look at the sequencing for the minor pieces in the same way, and then examine the detailed task list.

This process will take just a few moments if you use the major-minor piece mindmap. Simply put a number sequence (1, 2, 3, etc.) on each major piece, a separate number sequence on each minor piece within the major piece, and a separate number sequence on the tasks within the minor pieces.

Once sequence has been determined, the tasks can be entered on the appropriate project forms in sequence order.

STEP 5: DECIDE WHO IS RESPONSIBLE

The next element of planning is deciding who is going to take responsibility for each task. Use the task map and enter initials to indicate who is responsible for each piece, or task, of the project.

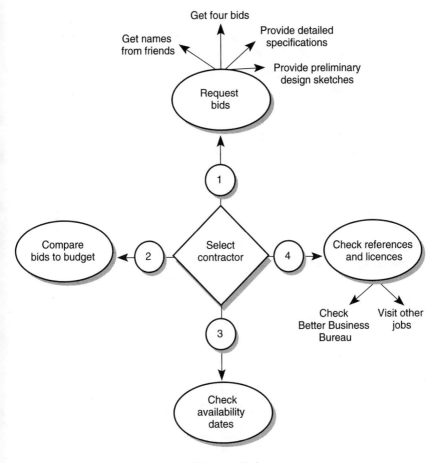

FIGURE 7-4
Prioritized Task Maps

This is a vital step. We are often effective at determining what needs to be done, but often not as clear about who is going to do it. This information makes the task map form an effective tool not only for planning but also for communicating. From this data, everyone can see his or her part, all the scheduling information, and the big picture. This puts an end to comments like "Gee, I thought you were going to do that" and "I didn't know my piece of the project was due today."

This information makes clear who is responsible for what

pieces of the project. In addition, it can help point out potential resource problems in case some people are overallocated during some or all of the project. This information can help clarify resource assignments, which can aid in negotiations that are sometimes necessary to ensure adequate availability of staff for the project.

The last column on the task map form is for the actual completion date. This is filled in as each task is completed and contains key information that will be vital as you evaluate projects (which we will discuss in Chapter 12, under the section on Close) and as you learn to improve and refine your estimating techniques.

There is one column left on the task map, next to the task priority column. This column will be used for status checking, using the following symbols:

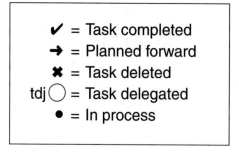

FIGURE 7-5
Status Symbols

STEP 6: DECIDE WHEN EACH TASK WILL BE DONE

Once we have detailed major and minor pieces and tasks, we are ready to start scheduling the project. One of the first and most important questions asked about a project is always when each task can be done. And it seems that no one ever wants something "whenever you can get around to it." People always want it PDS—pretty darn soon. These initials help us remember the three pieces of determining the *when* of a project:

- **Prioritizing**—determining which pieces of the project are vital to the success of the project
- **Duration**—projecting how much time each task will take
- **Schedule**—assigning a start date and target finish date for each major and minor piece and task

Prioritizing

The planning stage develops the ideal project—what we would really like to have happen. All too often, however, reality forces us to compromise. The time to have a clear understanding of what's critical and what's optional is at the beginning of the project, not when we're halfway through and have used up most of our resources. Therefore, we need to prioritize all of the tasks in terms of A, B, or C:

A indicates the highest priority, a task that is vital to the project's success and *must* be done. Most project pieces and tasks will fall into this category.
B indicates a task that is important to the quality of the project; it is not absolutely critical.
C indicates a task that would be nice, if resources permit.

While B's and C's are nice to have, they are not absolutely necessary to ensure a successful project completion. They are the tasks that contribute to the highest possible quality, but that, if absent, will not prevent the project from happening. The A's, on the other hand, are mandatory in order to successfully complete the project. In our home-remodeling example, laying the floor is an A. Installing carpeting might be a B because it is a high priority but could be done later. Buying that terrific Navajo rug for a centerpiece, however, would probably rate a C.

The task priority is entered on the second column from the left on the task map.

Duration

People often ask, "How do I estimate how long something will take?" There are two primary methods that can help with this: experience and effective estimating techniques. Of course, effective estimating techniques also come from experience. But it's not quite as circular as it seems.

While your first estimates may be little more than best guesses, eventually you will have enough experience to accurately project completion times for a wide variety of tasks. In Chapter 12, on closing and evaluating a project, we will talk more about comparing projected and actual times as a way of improving your skill in estimating times. Then, instead of doing best guesses, you'll be able to do best estimates. One way to improve your skill immediately is to do past-experience interviews. The purpose of this interview is to gain specific, task-related information from others who have done something similar in previous projects.

Past-experience interviews: Find the experts.

Even if the project you're working on is unique, there's a very good chance that others have done similar tasks while working on other projects. Those people can be a tremendous asset in knowing how long certain tasks might take, what resources would be required, and what the potential pitfalls might be. Here are some sample questions to ask:

- How long did the task take?
- What were some of the challenges you encountered?
- If you could go back and do it again, knowing what you know now, what would you do differently?

PROJECT TASK MAP

Project Title: _New Deck Back Patio_   Starting Date: _April_   Target Finish: _July 1_   Actual Finish: ___

Project Definition: _Replace old porch deck by July 4._   Project Expected Results: 1) _Within $3,000 budget._ 2) _Same design as old deck._ 3) _Natural color waterproof deck stain._

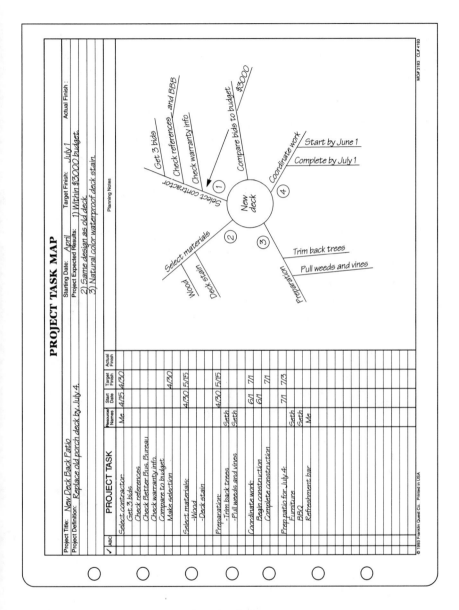

Planning Notes

✓ ABC	PROJECT TASK	Resource Names	Start Date	Target Finish	Actual Finish
	Select contractor:	Me	4/15	4/30	
	Get 3 bids				
	Check references				
	Check Better Bus. Bureau				
	Check warranty info				
	Compare to budget				
	Make selection			4/30	
	Select materials:		4/30	5/15	
	-Wood				
	-Deck stain				
	Preparation:		4/30	5/15	
	-Trim back trees	Seth			
	-Pull weeds and vines	Seth			
	Coordinate work:				
	Begin construction		6/1	7/1	
	Complete construction		6/1	7/1	
	Prep patio for July 4:		7/1	7/3	
	Furniture	Seth			
	BBQ	Seth			
	Refreshment bar	Me			

© 1993 Franklin Quest Co.   Printed in USA

MIOF 3183   CLF 4183

FIGURE 7-6
Example: Project Task Map—Deck

- Did the results differ from what you originally intended?
- Are there any common problems you think should be avoidable, and if so, what are they and how can I avoid them?

 Warning: Math formula ahead!
Skip if hazardous to mental health!

Using a Mathematical Formula to Estimate Time (Optional)

You may get many different opinions about how long a task might take. If the project budget is based on the estimated time, it may be important to estimate precisely how much time will be needed for the task. There are many mathematical approaches to time estimation. Perhaps the easiest to understand and use comes from *Project Management: From Idea to Implementation* by Marion Haynes. Here's the formula he suggests:

Tm = The most probable time
To = The optimistic (shortest) time within which only 1% of similar projects are completed
Tp = The pessimistic (longest) time within which 99% of similar projects are completed
Te = The calculated time estimate

$$Te = \frac{To + 4Tm + Te}{6}$$

This formula will help establish a standard deviation of the time estimate.

Once you have an estimate of how long each piece will take, you can use that information to calculate starting dates. You then enter this information on the task map form.

Example: You want to build a house. Most people tell you that it will take a year. One contractor says he can do it in six months, but a friend tells you that it took three years to complete his house. Here's your calculation:

$$Te = \frac{6 \text{ months} + 4 \times 1 \text{ year} + 3 \text{ years}}{6} = \frac{7.5 \text{ years}}{6} = 1.25 \text{ years}$$

SCHEDULING: FORWARD AND BACKWARD PLANNING

There are two approaches to project scheduling, depending on whether there is a fixed deadline or the project is open-ended.

Forward Planning

The forward-planning approach is used when no deadline has been set. Look at all of the individual pieces of the project and determine how long each will take. Then add the time frames together to determine a target deadline. Be sure to consider dependent tasks that cannot be started until the predecessor task is finished.

In the home-remodeling example, we would estimate the time necessary for each element of the project, then add them together to determine a deadline. If you go through that process and determine that the deadline is not acceptable, you then have to start balancing constraints. Do you add more resources? Reduce the scope or quality? Or can you find an innovative way to accomplish some of the tasks in less time?

Establishing a schedule will assure you that the project can be completed in a reasonable time, or it will stimulate you to rethink the project and make adjustments until the schedule meets your needs. Because you have already prioritized the tasks, you can look at all the B's and C's and determine which ones should be postponed or deleted.

Backward Planning

Use the backward-planning approach when you already have a deadline. The deadline may be a fixed date, such as a conference, wedding, or other special event, or it may be imposed by a project assignment, such as a budget that is due by a specific date.

Backward planning requires a step-by-step backing up from the deadline to determine the individual deadlines of each individual piece or task.

For example, the train-the-trainer program mentioned previously had a fixed deadline. To meet this deadline, all completed training materials needed to be received at the training location at least two days ahead of the training date. Allowing for adequate shipping time, we could back into our ship date. Then we estimated the number of days required to prepare the materials for shipping. This gave us a deadline for all of the training materials, including the guidebook, the video, and all other training materials. We followed this process until each significant piece had a scheduled due date. At that point all we needed was an estimate of how long each task would take so that we would also have a start date.

STEP 7: DETERMINE THE PROJECT BUDGET

Working through each of the previous steps is a major part of the budgeting process. We now know exactly what needs to be done and how much time it will take to do each part of the project. Costs can be assigned to each task and piece of the project. If this is the first time a project like this has been done, the budget may be nothing more than a best guess. If similar projects have been done, you may have precise cost information that can be plugged in. Once the project has been scheduled and budgeted, it is ready for any necessary approvals.

PROJECT APPROVAL AND ACCEPTANCE

Often at the end of the planning stage and prior to project implementation, a project review is required to make a go–no go decision based on the project plan. Sometimes revisions to the plan, especially in terms of resources, are required prior to project acceptance. I encourage a careful review of every project at this stage to make that decision. If a project is not likely to succeed, this is the last opportunity to kill it before the more expensive implementation stage is begun. This is also the time to consider postponing a project until a more appropriate time when more resources are available.

Some projects are highly complex and require more sophisticated techniques to manage the large number of tasks, resources, or people involved. The next chapter will show you a powerful tool to help manage large projects.

CHAPTER 8

PLAN

Additional Tools for More Complex Projects

COMING ATTRACTIONS:
- Guide to complex projects
- Project time lines
- Critical path

---

*If I had eight hours to chop down a tree,
I'd spend six sharpening my ax.*

—ABRAHAM LINCOLN

Good news—no matter how large or complex your projects are, the *process* of managing them never changes. Visualize, plan, implement, close—this process works for any size project.

What does change, however, is the set of tools used to manage the project. More complex projects require additional tools. This chapter adds a powerful tool to your project management tool kit. But before we get to that tool, we should have a working definition of "complex projects."

I generally break projects down into four levels of difficulty, depending on the number of tasks involved. Here's an outline of my project-complexity guidelines:

Level	No. of Tasks	Primary Tools
1	2 to 10	Day planner
2	10 to 35	Task map form
3	35 to 150	Project time line
4	150 and above	Computer technology

- **Level one** is basically a no-brainer. It requires only a few simple tasks that are obvious in terms of sequence. Detailing them into your day planner is all that is necessary.
- **Level two** projects require 10 to 35 tasks. They're not terribly difficult, but some help is needed to sort out the task detail, to determine the sequencing, and to be clear about who is doing what. These projects are ideal for the task map form discussed in Chapter 7.
- **Level three** is where it starts to get hairy. Level three projects can wake you up at 2:00 A.M. in a cold sweat, worrying about how in the world you are going to be able to pull it off—but that was before you had the VPIC model and all these cool management tools! The level three project has a lengthy task list with many task dependencies, and several other people are usually involved. You need some help getting this kind of project organized.
- **Level four** is reserved for huge, extremely sophisticated projects such as constructing a space shuttle or a building, launching a new product, or hosting the Olympics. While level four projects are beyond the scope of this book, effective management of them would use the Visualize-Plan-Implement-Close model, and they would incorporate the tools from all the other levels.

Project complexity has much more to do with how many tasks are involved, how interdependent they are, and how many people are involved than with the time period of the project. A six-week project involving hundreds of tasks will be much more difficult to manage than a two-year project with only a few tasks. However, the time line of the project is a critical component of complex tasks.

PROJECT TIME LINES (GANTT CHARTS)

Controlling a complex project requires an additional tool—the project time line, commonly called a Gantt chart. This is a visual guide that shows the relationships between tasks and time. It was created by Henry Gantt around the turn of the century to help manage some of the early industrial projects. In spite of age, the chart is still an effective and easy-to-use tool that can be easily understood by most members of a project team.

Project time lines provide important information about the project in visual terms most people can understand. They are invaluable for keeping everyone involved on the project aware of deadlines and interrelationships and dependencies of tasks.

Some of the other, more sophisticated tools, such as PERT (Program Evaluation Review Technique) charts, are difficult to understand without specialized training in their use. While they may be necessary on very large and sophisticated projects, because only highly trained members of the team are able to use and understand them, they don't provide the high level of communication between team members that project time lines do. Therefore, we will focus on project time lines and leave the PERT charts to more sophisticated project management texts.

Project time lines communicate task and time relationships visually.

The major advantage of a Gantt chart is that, in charting the time frame for each individual task and project chunk, it provides a visual outline of the total amount of time a project

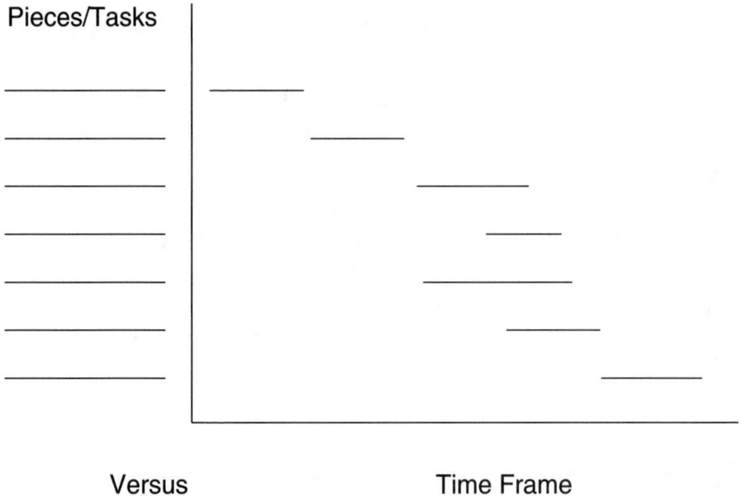

Pieces/Tasks

Versus   Time Frame

FIGURE 8-1
Example: Gantt Chart

will take. Laying out the entire project in this fashion often reveals areas where changes in resources or techniques can save time on a project. Anytime you identify tasks that can be done in a parallel fashion, rather than being dependent on one another, you have an opportunity to reduce the total time the project will take. That generally means reduced cost or less time to project completion, or both.

I have two large clients in an industry where the *average* length of time of one of their projects is fourteen years. Every single day they can shave from their project time line results in a savings in excess of fifty thousand dollars! It may not be worth quite that much to you or your company to reduce the total time of a project, but the savings could still be significant in customer satisfaction, freeing up valuable resources or reduced cost.

Gantt charts also point out significant bottlenecks or places where even small delays could have a major impact on the project deadline. It provides a detailed picture of tasks as well as a big picture of the total project. This is vital in helping each team member see the consequences that may occur if his or her piece of the project is delayed. The project time line should be present at every project review meeting (these meetings will be discussed in Chapter 9).

There are several ways to produce a Gantt chart—paper and pencil, a computer spreadsheet, or project management software. We'll discuss the creation of Gantt charts in detail, but first a word about available software.

PROJECT MANAGEMENT SOFTWARE

In the past few years, many project management software programs have been developed. Many of these packages, however, are overkill for the average project manager. While they are extremely robust in their capabilities, they're not particularly user-friendly. I'm always hearing stories about expensive software that was abandoned because it was just too complex.

While the software can help with many tasks, there is much it will *not* do for you. Software will not ensure that you have a clear project vision to begin with. It won't break your project down into major and minor pieces, nor will it detail your tasks for you. It won't tell you which tasks are dependent on others or which tasks can be performed in a parallel fashion.

If *you* program all of that information into the computer correctly, then the computer can help you graphically present the project, share the information with others (via printouts, floppy disks, or network capabilities), easily make changes to the original and perform "what if" scenarios. The first step with any software or manual process, however, is having a clear understanding of the project and the interaction of the tasks.

With this understanding, software can be an indispensable

resource tool on large projects (in excess of a hundred tasks). My experience is that, for small projects, I spend more time managing the software than managing the project.

If you have abandoned your project software, you may want to retrieve it, blow the dust off, and try it again now that you have a process to follow. If you are interested in purchasing software, research your choices carefully. There are too many choices available for me to review in the scope of this text, but the features and prices range dramatically, from the $25 quickie variety (I have never found one of these to be worth the price) up to price tags of hundreds of dollars. Be clear about what you need, ask associates in your particular industry for their opinion of various programs, and if possible, get demo disks before you invest. Above all, purchase your software from a reputable company with a return policy in case you test it and dislike it or find it inappropriate for your needs.

Or you may prefer the simpler and certainly less expensive approach, using pencil and paper. Regardless of whether you're using a software or paper approach, the technique for creating a project time line is the same. You can create your own project time line form or use a printed form such as the timetable form from Franklin Covey. (See Appendix A.)

CREATING A PROJECT TIME LINE

The following gives you a step-by-step guide for creating a project time line or timetable using a form created on a spreadsheet or preprinted form such as the one shown in Figure 8-2. Here are some common definitions and symbols.

PROJECT TIME LINE TERMS _____

Dependent task: A task that cannot begin until its predecessor tasks are complete.

Predecessor task: A task that must be done before other, dependent, tasks can be begun.

Duration: The amount of time a task takes.

Parallel task: A task that can be done concurrently with one or more other tasks.

Slack, or float, time: The extra time available to complete a task without delaying the start of subsequent tasks.

Critical path: The series of tasks that must occur as scheduled for a project to finish on schedule; tasks on the critical path have no slack time. If a task on the critical path is delayed, the project will be delayed.

Step 1: Enter major and minor pieces and their respective tasks in the column marked Pieces/Tasks, *in sequence order,* as demonstrated in your mindmap notes. Enter the name of the person responsible for the each piece and/or task, or the necessary equipment or resources required, in the column marked Resources/Names.

Step 2: Prioritize the pieces and tasks as follows:

A. Vital to project success.
B. Important but optional. Not required for project success.
C. Optional. Nice if time and resources permit.

Step 3: Fill in the column labeled "Duration"—for instance, 6 wk; 2 D; 4 mo. A short project may be tracked in terms of hours or days, while a longer project would be in terms of weeks or months.

Project Timetable

| Project Title: Advanced Security System | Project Number: 0429 | Project Manager: Jean Smith | Target Finish: Mar. 1998 | Actual Finish: |

Time Span by Day Week Month (circle one)

Item No.	✓	A B C	Pieces/Tasks	Duration	Predecessors	Start Date	Target Finish	Actual Finish	Est. Costs	Act.	Resources/ Names
		A	1.0 Product Research								
			1.1 Define Technical Specs								
		A	2.0 Product Development								
			2.1 Design								
			2.2 Test/Revise								
			2.3 Final Dev. and Release								
		A	3.0 Marketing								
			3.1 Packaging								
			3.2 Catalog Piece								
			3.3 Brochure								
			3.4 Product Announcement								
		A	4.0 Training								
			4.1 Sales								
			4.2 Technical Support								

FIGURE 8-2
Project Timetable with Major and Minor Pieces

Step 4: Determine if the project is best managed with forward or backward planning (see Chapter 7). This will determine whether you start at the end of the project and work backward or start at the beginning and work forward. Task time is indicated by a horizontal line illustrating the task duration (see "Duration" column) and the dependency relationship (see "Predessors" column). For example, if task number two is dependent upon task number one, and task number one took four weeks, task number two would start in week five (using a weekly time span). Fill in the time line with a horizontal line to indicate the amount of time allotted to each task. (Note that major and minor pieces are summary bars whose length is determined by the total time for all tasks included in that piece). A vertical connecting line may be helpful to show dependencies. Here are some common time line (Gantt Chart) symbols.

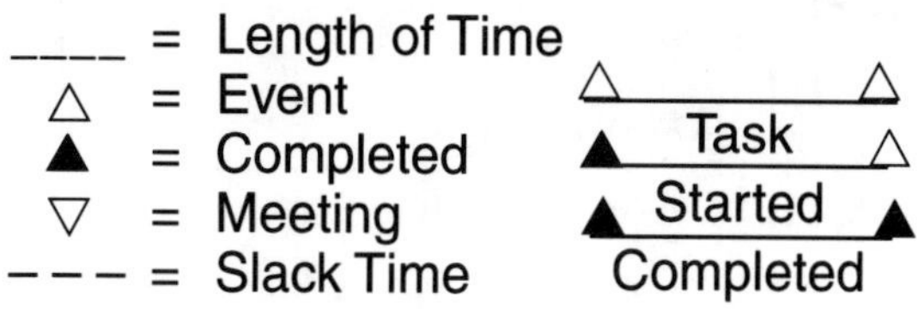

____	=	Length of Time
△	=	Event
▲	=	Completed
▽	=	Meeting
− − −	=	Slack Time

△ _____ △
▲ **Task** △
▲ **Started** ▲
Completed

FIGURE 8-3

Gantt Chart symbols. Color coding: Highlight tasks on the critical path. Use color highlighters (weekly or daily) to indicate tasks that are early, late, or on time.

Step 5: Use the information from the time line to go back and fill in the start date and target finish date for each task and piece. Track and record the actual finish date to aid in the project evaluation.

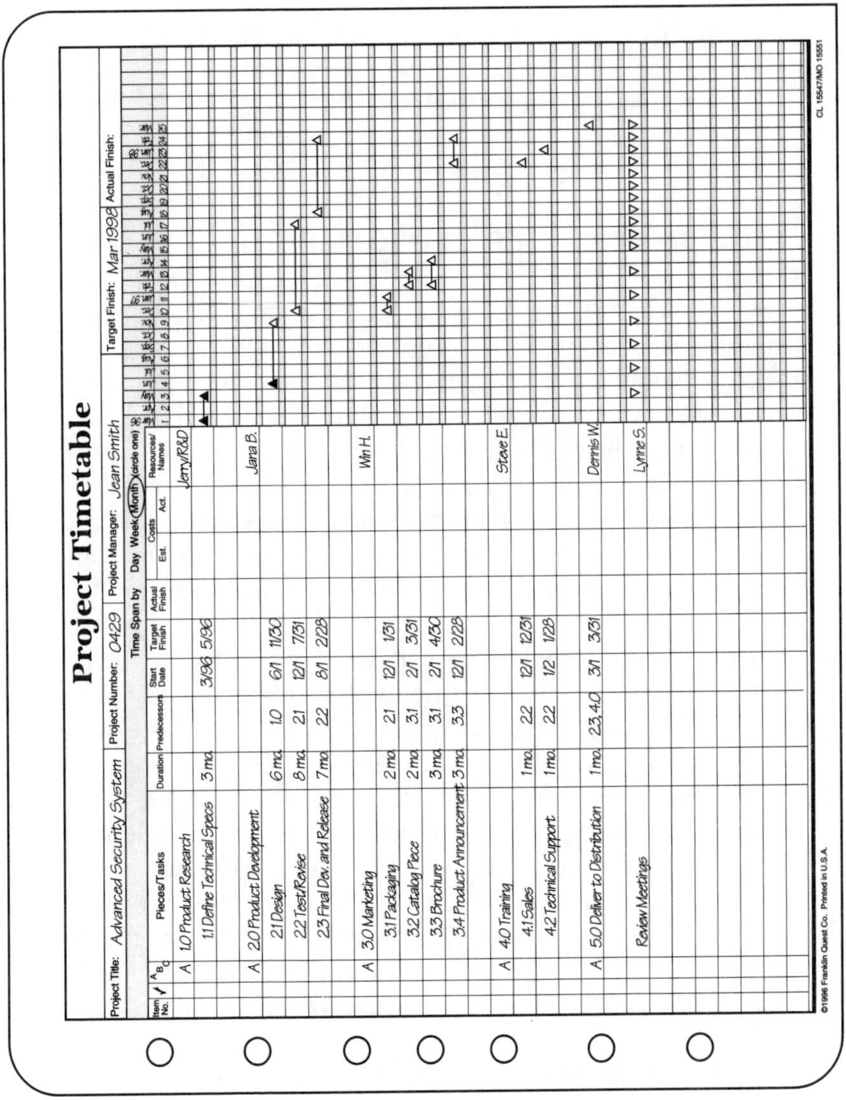

FIGURE 8-4
Project Timetable—Completed

Step 6: Determine the project budget: Estimate a cost for each piece and task, as appropriate. Use a spreadsheet if necessary.

HIGHLIGHTING THE CRITICAL PATH

Once the Gantt Chart is completed, it is important to understand the critical path on the project. Highlighting the critical path is helpful to every member of the project team. Some tasks will have some slack or float time, meaning there is some flexibility in their time frame. Other tasks are on the critical path, meaning that if any one of them is delayed, it will delay the succeeding dependent tasks, and consequently the project completion will be delayed. An effective project manager watches the time line and monitors the critical path carefully.

For example, if task number 3.3 is delayed by one month, what is the effect on the project? What if it is delayed by five months? Keep in mind that no matter how much slack time may be available, every task is potentially on the critical path.

Now look at task number 1.1. What will be the result if this task is delayed by one month? Even though this delay would occur much earlier in the project, the result would be more dramatic because this task is on the critical path. At least you know this information and can manage it accordingly. Perhaps the information can aid in negotiating a different priority being placed on the project and adjusting resources. Participants and stakeholders are at least aware of the results of such a delay.

I learned how to use project time lines when I was managing projects in an engineering company. We found this technique most helpful at project team meetings. We would post the project time line on the wall and use a yellow highlighter to show our progress on each task. It became a real reinforcement to be able to visually see progress. It was also helpful in coaxing the natural procrastinators in the group to keep up.

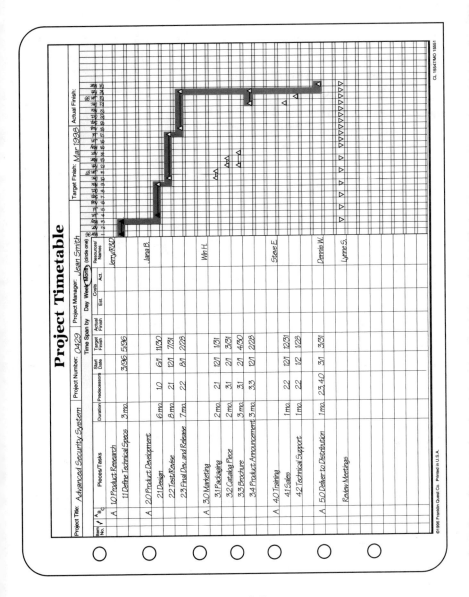

FIGURE 8-5
Timetable with Critical Path Highlighted

The engineers finally caught on; they did not want to come into the project war room and see that their task was the one that was holding everyone else up. It was a gentle but effective way to break the procrastination habit.

Once the planning process is done and all the required approvals have been obtained, we're ready to move on to the implementation stage.

IMPLEMENT

Coordinating with Your Day Planner

---

*You can't have a better tomorrow
if you are thinking about yesterday all the time.*

—CHARLES F. KETTERING

Finally we get to the place where most people start—the actual implementation of the project, the doing. Implementation is the carrying out of a plan using appropriate tools to monitor progress. If we have chosen a project based on our values and planned it carefully, implementation will be simplified. But this is still a critical stage of project completion. Our ability to keep the project on track while adjusting to the inevitable changes in requirements, resource availability, time estimates, and so forth depends on our ability to use the implementation tools and strategies.

The implementation stage consists of two primary strategies:

- Coordination with day planner
- Coordination and communication with other people

Coordination and control of your projects with your day planner will be discussed in this chapter. Coordination and communication with other people will be discussed in Chapter 10.

TIME ACTIVATING: COORDINATING YOUR PROJECT WITH YOUR DAY PLANNER

Your day planner is the fundamental tool of project management. Regardless of which planner you use, it should tell you *where* you should be and *what* you should be working on at any given moment. At Franklin Quest, this is called Time Activation. To *Time-Activate* information is to select the appropriate day and time to follow up on or take action on project-related tasks. Time Activation answers three questions:

1. *What* needs to be done?
2. *When* does it need to occur?
3. *Where* is the information stored?

PROJECT TIME-ACTIVATION STEPS _____

- Set up project tab in your day planner.
- Time-Activate project into daily task list.
- Make project appointments.

STEP 1: SET UP PROJECT TAB IN YOUR DAY PLANNER

When you begin a new project, the first thing to do is to set up a project tab page in your day planner. All your project management documentation will be stored behind this tab. This, of course, assumes it is a significant project in terms of size and not a project so simple that a series of tasks can be scheduled directly into your planner without the need for any additional tools. Many projects are that simple. However, assuming that this is a significant project that will require some additional tools, setting up the project tab is the place to start. Behind this tab should go the project task map form, timetable forms and other chosen project forms.

To avoid any unnecessary duplication of efforts, do not enter project tasks onto the prioritized daily task list. Instead, simply time-activate the project into your daily task list, as described below.

STEP 2: TIME-ACTIVATE PROJECT INTO DAILY TASK LIST

When you're ready to Time-Activate your project into your daily task list you want to create a Time-Activation reference that will immediately transmit the answers to the three Time-Activation questions.

Questions	Time-Activation Reference	Example
1. What needs to be done?	Project title	Remodel
2. When does the next step need to occur?	Daily page	June 2
3. Where is the information stored?	Project location	PT3

This example shows that you are going to work on the Remodel project on June 2 and that the project information is located in project tab 3. The entry on your project task list for June 2 would be "Remodel (PT3)." But that's not enough.

TAF: The Project Two-Step

Unlike everyday tasks, project tasks are not done when you do them. Huh? . . . Remember, projects are different. They're not done until the entire project is done. Just as important as doing the remodel tasks scheduled for June 12 is determining when the next tasks are scheduled. Otherwise you'd just do the task scheduled for today and then forget about the project until someone started yelling. This reminder process is called Time-Activating Forward (TAF). So there is another piece needed to make the Time-Activation reference complete—a TAF reminder. Here's what the entire Time-Activation reference looks like:

(title)	(location)	/TAF

In the example for June 2, the entry "Remodel (PT3)/TAF" tells me to go to project tab 3 (the one I have assigned to my remodeling project). My task map or timetable form tells me there are two tasks that need to be done today. Once those actions are taken, nothing else needs to be done on the project until July 1, so I will enter the Time-Activation reference on the daily task list for July 1. *Then* I get to check off today's item on my daily planner. Finally, an endorphin!☺

The location reference shows you which project tab contains all of the current information you need to manage that project effectively. The task map or timetable form, located in the same section, gives you the details of which tasks you need to work on for the day. All you do is look at the date column to see what needs doing today. Check each task off on this form as you complete it. At the end of each work session, look at the forms to determine what needs to be done next and when. Go into your day planner to the page for the next day you need to work on the project. Time-Activate the project on that day's page, exactly as you did before. You have just ensured that the work won't slip through the cracks by completing the Time-Activate Forward (TAF) portion of the project reference.

This simple process gives you two benefits: a check mark endorphin for the activities you completed and the right to forget about the project because you have it scheduled forward to show up at the proper time on your daily task list. This is a major stress reducer. You don't have to worry about it. You have ensured that it is going to come up when it is supposed to. You can relax and go on to your next priority.

Referencing Other Project Files

In this system, parentheses refer you to files or information sources. Your project tabs typically house the *project management* information you need to help you effectively manage a particular project. However, you may have other files set up for some projects. The parentheses are used on your daily task list or project forms to refer to any specific file. When I was writing this book, my daily task list often looked like this:

A1. Planning and solitude
A2. Book (Implmnt)/TAF

This reference tells me that my second highest priority today is to work on the implementation chapter of the book. The parentheses refer me to the computer file titled "Implement." The reference also helps me to be specific about what part of the project needs work. If you are working on a large project, parentheses are great to refer to specific major or minor pieces, filenames, or information locations.

STEP 3: MAKE PROJECT APPOINTMENTS

Projects are generally long-term important but not short-term urgent. Working on them usually requires more concentration and effort than working on regular, non-project-related tasks. And since most of us have enough regular work to do every day before we even begin to think about our projects, we generally need more than just a project notation on our daily task list, even if it is an A! One way to create the time we need for our projects is to make actual appointments. Estimate the amount of time you will need to complete a project activity and actually block it out in your appointment schedule for that day (see Figure 9-1).

If you need a two-hour session to work on a project, find your best two-hour slot and block it out in your appointment calendar, the same way you would if you had a commitment to attend a meeting for those hours. If this is a personal project, you can do the same thing in your off-work hours.

A woman in one of my workshops once looked at me aghast and asked, "Can you do that?" *Yes,* you can do that. In fact you need to do that in order to effectively bring project work back into the day along with your other daily tasks. Otherwise we will fill our day with the short-term urgent items and our projects will never get done, or we'll do them during our evenings and weekends, taking away from our other values and any hope of leading a balanced life.

Defending Your Project Appointments

Your project appointments need to carry as much weight as your other time commitments. Because of my travel schedule, I spend only a few days a month in the office. On those days I generally get to the office by 8:00 A.M. The phone is ringing and people are at my door by 8:05. I always do my planning and solitude at home because I would never get it done at the office. And without that planning, I'd go home at the end of

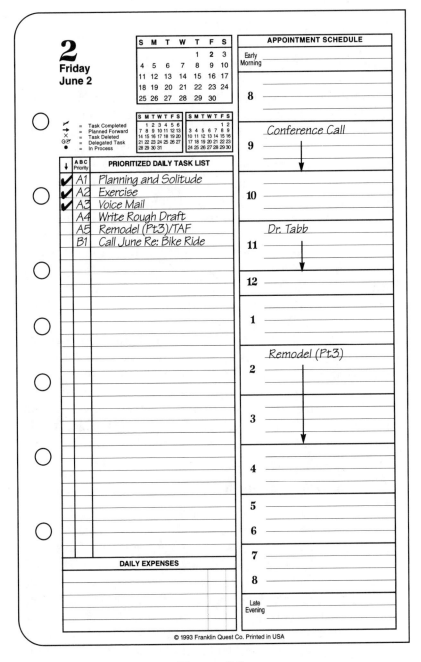

FIGURE 9-1
Block Appointment Time for Work on Key Projects

the day exhausted, with no idea of whether or not I'd accomplished what needed to be done.

But if I've done my planning and decided in advance that I need to work on a project from 10:00 to 12:00, here's what often happens. Don, my boss, comes to me and says, "Lynne, glad you're back. A lot happened while you were away, and we need to spend some time together today. When can we meet?"

I look at my day planner and respond, "I have a meeting from nine to ten, a commitment from ten to twelve, and a meeting at two. Other than that, Don, what works for you?" Notice I did not say, "I am working on a project from ten to twelve." If I had, I am sure you could imagine the response: "Work on the project later and see me at ten." Instead, I said I had a commitment. It *is* a commitment. A commitment to my project priorities, my work, and myself. I feel no guilt about handling it this way.

So what do I do when Don says, "Sorry, Lynne. I have a busy day today; ten o'clock is the only opening I have"? Keep in mind that the day planner is flexible. It works for *us;* we don't work for it. I look at my day planner, move the project work session to three o'clock, and pencil Don in at ten. While I had to change my schedule to adapt to my boss's schedule, I didn't fail to carve out a couple of hours to work on my project.

Dealing with Interruptions

Into every day a lot of interruptions fall. Dealing effectively with those interruptions can be the ultimate challenge for project managers. Here are a few suggestions that have been gleaned from hundreds of project management workshops:

1. **Prioritize the interruption.** Just because it interrupts you does not mean it is automatically an A item. If a phone call or visitor brings you something to handle, take a brief moment and evaluate the importance of the item. Write it down on your daily task list and determine its priority. If it is a B or a C, you can go back to working

on your project and take care of the task in its proper time. If it is a legitimate A, determine if it is a "drop-everything, do-me-now A" or an A you can schedule in with other A's that need to be taken care of before the end of the day. If so, they don't need to interrupt the time you've scheduled for your project.

2. **The office swap.** Swap offices with another person at work who also needs a couple of hours to work on a project. Any visitors who come to that person's office aren't looking for you. They are looking for the other person and will leave quickly. When the phone rings, you have two choices: answer it, take a quick message, and get back to work on your project; or let voice mail or an assistant take messages. When the two of you go back to your own offices, you can quickly respond to phone messages and proceed with your day.

3. **Work in a conference or meeting room.** Spending a few hours in a private room with no phone is an even better way to get some work done. Frequently these rooms are available just by showing up or signing up.

4. **Leave the office.** Best yet, when possible, leave the office. When I was working on the development of our seminar guidebook there were three of us who were finding it almost impossible to work at the office. Someone in the building was always wanting one or more of us, so the interruptions were magnified by three. Finally, we started arranging two- and three-hour meetings at a local coffee shop. It was a perfect work environment. Our guidebook was designed almost entirely at the Salt Lake Roasting Company.

Much of the early work for this book was developed as Joyce and I sat in the finest coffee shops in Portland, Oregon. We'd brainstorm and drink coffee, and when we hit a lull, we'd prowl through a bookstore or an office supply store until the ideas started flowing again. Then we'd head for the next coffee shop to capture the ideas. We also had an extremely productive session sitting in a

Brighton, Utah, ski lodge with our portable computers. If the time is productive and the quality of the work good, you can justify working in wonderful places.

5. **Create a home office.** Even if you work for a company, consider yourself "Me Incorporated," a wonderful idea of Denis Waitley's. If you consider yourself your own incorporated business, it's easier to recognize that investing in the number one asset of that business (you!) makes good business sense. This philosophy states that you are now choosing to lease your services to your present employer and that, at some time in the future, you may choose to lease your services to another employer or to become self-employed. Therefore, it makes sense to invest in the continued growth and development of your knowledge, skills, talents, and abilities as a way of improving your personal net worth. Ben Franklin said, "If you always put the money from your purse into your mind, your mind will always replace the money in your purse."

Because of this belief in investing in myself, I have dedicated a room in my house to an office with a desk, filing system, personal computer, printer, fax, and two-line phone. In fact, I have a far nicer office at home than I do at work. This makes it possible to get better-quality work done at home than I could ever get done at the office. My home office also allows me to accommodate my preference for weird work hours. However, working at home requires a lot of self-motivation and self-discipline as well as support from family and friends. Otherwise you may find yourself running errands, stopping to do "just one load of laundry," and being on call every moment. You also need to be aware that sometimes with a home office it is difficult to stop working and "be home," especially for those prone to workaholism. If you can manage these challenges effectively, however, the rewards are tremendous. The quality of your work can improve, and thus your opportunities for growth, development, and advancement.

6. **Use a Do Not Disturb sign.** When you do need to remain at the office, don't neglect the standard Please Do Not Disturb sign. You can write this out, post it on your office or cubicle door, and as long as it is not there all the time, it will most likely be respected. Be as specific as possible. You might try this on a sign with a pencil hanging from it and a sign-up sheet taped to the bottom: "Deadline pending: Unless it is urgent, please do not disturb. Leave a message, and I will call you as soon as I can." Then sign it with a big "Thanks!"

Try brainstorming in your own organization to come up with suggestions for effectively spending dedicated time working on a project. But most importantly, stop waiting for a time when you can spend three or four uninterrupted hours working on a project. It may not be impossible but it's definitely improbable! Break the project down into more manageable pieces and work on it when you have twenty to thirty minutes free. This is especially helpful when you have a ten o'clock appointment that doesn't show up till ten-thirty.

Organize your projects so they can be accomplished in twenty- to thirty-minute chunks.

FORGOTTEN ITEMS AND AFTERTHOUGHTS

As you start to work on the project, you will undoubtedly think of things that you need to do that were not thought of in the planning process. Those tasks can be easily added to the bottom of your project task map form. Record the start date and target finish date for that task. Then Time-Activate the project reference into your day planner if the date is before your next scheduled work session. If it is not, you don't need to Time-Activate it now. You will do so during a future work session.

Remember, in spite of the fact that we originally went to some effort to list tasks sequentially into the project task map or timetable form, it is the start date, not the placement in the list, that determines when a task will be done. Listing things sequentially will help you see and understand the flow of events. Sequencing is extremely important and helpful with even more complex projects, but as long as you are monitoring the start-date column on the form carefully, adding a few items to the bottom of the list should not pose a problem.

Another way to handle forgotten items and afterthoughts is to enter the new task directly onto your daily task list on the date it needs to be done. I do this, however, only if I am sure that this information is not needed on the original project form. In other words, if there will never be another project just like this or there will never be a need to share this project information with anyone else, and, therefore, the fact that this task is missing from the original documentation will never pose a problem to a future project. The best practice is to keep all the project tasks referenced on the project task map form or timetable form rather than dribbled throughout the daily task list pages.

TYING PROJECTS INTO THE MONTHLY CALENDAR PAGE

The final step in coordinating projects back into your day planner is to put vital project information onto the monthly calendar page. This page is your general overview, not just to projects, but to your life. You may plan out an individual project well, but if it interferes with other projects or events in your life, you have not done yourself any favors. We need to see the big picture.

Enter major commitment dates and due dates on the monthly calendar. Also, show scheduled project review meetings. Using the monthly calendar is the key to controlling your

MONTHLY CALENDAR

SUN.	MON.	TUES.	WED.	THURS.	FRI.	SAT.
	10-11 Review Meeting (Pt6)	**1**	**2**	**3** 9-11: Staff Meeting	**4** 2-3 Review Mtng (Pt5) Camping	**5** Family Camping Trip
6	**7** 10-11: Review Mtng (Pt6) 1-3 Training Meeting	**8** 3: Dr. Tabb	**9** 2-4 Mtng w/Don	**10** 9-11: Staff Meeting	**11** 2-3 Review Mtng (Pt5)	**12** Horse- back Riding
13	**14** 10-11 Review Meeting (Pt6) 3-5 (Pt6)	**15** 2-5 (Pt5)	**16** ABC Project -Key event (Pt5)	**17** 9-11: Staff Meeting	**18** Family Dinner	**19**
20 Horse- back Riding w/Seth	**21** 10-11 Review Meeting (Pt6)	**22** 9: Flight to DC	**23** Balti- more	**24** Wash DC	**25** DC 6:40 Flight home (8-1)	**26** Horse- back Riding
27	**28** 9-3 (Pt6)	**29** 10-4 (Pt6)	**30** XYZ Project Due (Pt6)	**31** 9-11: Staff Meeting 2-3 Review Meeting (Pt5)		9-3 Bike-A- Thon

FIGURE 9-2
Tie Projects to Your Monthly Calendar

month. If you see a project deadline during the month and you know you have a few days' worth of work to do to prepare for that deadline, block out the time on your calendar for those work sessions.

This process has been extremely important to me. Years ago it was apparent that I had crossed over the line into workaholism. I had gradually taken more and more work home in the evenings, then the weekends, and suddenly I looked at my life and realized it was very one-sided. As a single parent, I had been caught between the economic realities of life and my parental responsibilities. I looked at my son, Seth, and realized he wasn't getting any younger. Suddenly I imagined him off at college and me sitting home thinking to myself, "Dang [or some other expletive], I sure wish we'd spent more time together."

Somehow I had to find time to do my work and spend time with my son. The monthly calendar page became *the* tool that helped me bring balance back into my life. Like an effective budget, it helped me see and eliminate some of the events in my life that were not important to my value system. I began cutting back on my travel and teaching schedule to create more balance between my values and financial structure, and in time, I felt more balance in my life. I wouldn't have been able to do this without the additional time and productivity I gained by carefully planning my projects and consistently entering work sessions into my month. Soon I was getting things done without taking my projects home every weekend.

The significant thing about the monthly calendar page is that it will tell you, every day of every month, how you are doing. If you look at the calendar and don't see projects and activities that reflect your values showing up on a regular basis, it isn't working yet. This page is about your life, not just about your projects. On this page, you will be able to see whether you have created balance in your life.

As a side note, by the time this book is published, my son will be in college. I am very proud of the relationship we have developed and the quality time we have spent with each other, thanks to the increased effectiveness I gained from this system.

PROJECT "BOSS"

While it may stretch the definition of the word "project" just a bit, I even consider my boss a project. When I mention this in class it gets a supportive chuckle of agreement and not many challenges. Try setting up a project tab for your boss. That's where you'll keep a record of all conversations, assignments, and commitments. It works, and it's especially helpful around review time to have a history of all the meetings you've had as well as the objectives and assignments you have received and completed throughout the year.

After attending one of my workshops, my boss came to the next staff meeting and showed us his project management notebook—with a tab for each of us in the meeting. He explained that we were his projects, and each of us had our own project tab so he could track projects, conversations, and meetings with us.

SYSTEM ADVANTAGES

There are several advantages to this system of coordinating a project into your day planner. Perhaps the major advantage is that every time you work on a project, you not only see today's detail, you also see the big picture. You get a quick take on what has happened so far. Is everything on track? What is coming up in the future? Is everything set up for future events? Are any changes or adjustments necessary?

Another major advantage of this system is that it accommodates many projects at a time, since rarely do any of us work on only one project. Our project challenges, it seems, come from all the projects we're working on simultaneously, not to mention all the other non-project-oriented tasks that need to be accomplished in a day. Often people tell me that they have a normal eight-hour workday; *then* they have their project work to do. This is usually an indicator that project work has spilled over into the other areas of life—after hours. This system helps you coordinate all those projects back into your daily life where they can be prioritized according to your values and objectives.

Another benefit is the documentation that is created by this system. With all the information and details filed by project, it is easy to go back to completed projects to find out how something was done, who did a specific task, how much an activity cost, or how long it took. An example of how important this can be happened not long ago when I was assigned a new boss. We were in one of our early meetings together discussing ways to reduce product costs within my department. As I reviewed the figures he had been given by our accounting department, I immediately realized that the figures were incorrect. I had been a part of the original product design team three years earlier, and the numbers he was working with looked as if we were being dramatically overcharged. I said, "Hold on for just a moment; I need to get something," and I excused myself from his office.

I walked to my office, took the appropriate project storage binder from my bookshelf, found the project tab, and within a few moments found the meeting planner page from the team meeting three years earlier when we were given the product quotes. By the time I returned to his office, no more than two or three minutes had passed. I put the page of notes in front of him. He was blown away at my ability to retrieve such detailed information so quickly.

With my notes, we were able to have the accounting department correct this rather serious error. (My boss also came to my next public seminar to learn the system I was teaching. That's what got him using the project notebooks for his staff and projects.)

In the next chapter, we will discuss how to coordinate and communicate with other people who are vital to the success of our projects.

CHAPTER 10

IMPLEMENT

Coordinating and Communicating

with Other People

C O M I N G A T T R A C T I O N S :
- ARC delegation
- Project review meetings
- TULE meetings

Destiny is not a matter of chance,
it is a matter of choice;
it is not a thing to be waited for:
it is a thing to be achieved.

—WILLIAM JENNINGS BRYAN

Projects are seldom one-person affairs. In the planning stage, we generally identify many tasks that need to be done by other people. Often those folks were not part of the planning process, so they do not share the vision of the project team. They also may have a full plate long before you approach them to add another piece to their pile. But we've been hammered about how important it is to delegate, and by gosh, we're going to delegate.

DELEGATION, THE OLD WAY

After a planning session, we come away motivated to get the job done and ready to jump into action. We approach someone who's been identified as the right person to perform a task, explain the task briefly and tell him or her we need the task done by Monday. Then we're off to the next person to explain the next task. Progress is being made . . . we've delegated all the tasks and we start working on our own action items. We get called into a meeting on Monday and when we get back to the first person on Tuesday morning, we find that the task hasn't been finished. As a matter of fact, all the materials haven't even been ordered. Other tasks depended on this one being finished, so suddenly the entire project is slipping. We're angry, frustrated, and disillusioned with the person and with this whole project management business.

Stop. The problem isn't with the person who didn't complete the task, nor is it with project management. The problem is that we used a form of delegation I call "dump and run." This is seldom effective and leaves few choices other than to take a negative personnel action, do the task ourselves, or both. What we really want is to delegate a task in a way that guarantees that it will be completed successfully and on time.

ARC: THE EFFECTIVE WAY TO DELEGATE

Effective delegation is a two-way street. It's an arc of responsibility for the task, a bridge of communication that links two people. Delegation involves more than turning the responsibility for a task over to someone else. That person must accept the task, have the authority necessary to get the task done, and commit to achieving the task in the manner and time frame necessary. This mutual agreement is called the Delegation ARC.

- **Authority.** The person doing the task must have the authority to accomplish it, especially if the task requires additional resources, reprioritization of time, and so on.
- **Responsibility.** Responsibility for the end result is shared by both parties.
- **Commitment.** The person who accepts the task commits to achieving the end result in the agreed-upon time frame.

If any one of these elements is missing, the delegation will be unsuccessful. In your planning sessions, you identified people to do specific tasks. In each case, an assumption was made that the person who took responsibility for the task would also have the authority to marshal the necessary resources (including the person's own time) to complete the task. What was not addressed was commitment. Delegating is not a one-way activity. I cannot delegate to you. We—you and I—can agree to delegate the task to you. Your acceptance of the task and commitment to accomplish it the way it needs to be done in the allotted time is just as important as my releasing it to you.

So how do we build this commitment? The same way we developed commitment and enthusiasm in the primary project team—by building on personal values and developing a clear picture of the end result. You don't have to go through the entire planning process with each person responsible for a task, but you do have the perfect tool to show the overview of the project and how the task fits into the whole—the project task map or a Gantt chart.

By sharing either of these forms, the person can see the expected results and the big picture view of the project. The person who takes on the task has to catch the project vision at least to the extent necessary to successfully complete his portion of it. He needs a clear description of the task to be done and the expected results which will determine that the task has been successfully completed. If it is more than one simple task, you may want to work through a project task map form for the delegated activities.

Once the task is delegated, the responsibility for its completion is still a shared responsibility, which means that you need to agree upon a follow-up process. Regardless of how clear the beginning of the delegation process is, monitoring and follow-up are always required, because things change. When change is viewed as a realistic part of any project, members of the task team can look for new solutions and opportunities rather than worrying about who's to blame. Agreeing on a follow-up process at the beginning of the project is an acknowledgment that changes will occur and that you will work together to adapt to them.

DAY PLANNER COORDINATION OF DELEGATED TASKS

Your day planner is an invaluable tool in coordinating delegated tasks. Two symbols are used in the day planner to help ensure that delegated items never again slip through the cracks. One is the delegation symbol, and the other is a symbol to remind you to follow up with someone. These symbols can be used on the daily task list or any of the project task forms.

For example, during my planning and solitude session, I realize that Sara can generate a special sales report. I put Sara's initials on my project task map next to that task (or on the daily task list, if it's not a project task). Later I meet with Sara, clearly explain the project and task, the expected results, and the due date. Sara agrees to complete the task, so I put a circle in the status column to tell me that the task has been delegated.

The next step is the one that will ensure success: Sara and I discuss a follow-up plan. I might say something like this: "Sara, this sales report needs to be ready for the meeting

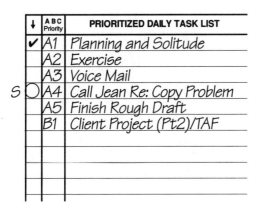

↓	ABC Priority	PRIORITIZED DAILY TASK LIST
✔	A1	Planning and Solitude
	A2	Exercise
	A3	Voice Mail
S ◯	A4	Call Jean Re: Copy Problem
	A5	Finish Rough Draft
	B1	Client Project (Pt2)/TAF

FIGURE 10-1
Delegation Symbol

next Monday. When can you and I touch base to make sure there aren't any snags?"

Sara might then say, "I'll know Thursday night if I can get the printout, so why don't you call me Friday morning?"

I'd reply, "Thanks, I'll plan on calling you at ten o'clock." Then I Time-Activate that step into my day planner.

Most of us have experienced being overcontrolled and "micromanaged" during our careers. Because of those unpleasant experiences, we sometimes fail to follow up on delegated tasks because we don't want to do the same thing to others.

The ARC style of delegation is different in two important ways. First, we created a shared vision with Sara by explaining the project vision to her, showing her the task map, pointing out the role of the task within the project, and explaining the time constraints for the deadline. Second, we release responsibility to Sara without removing our support. We let her know that we're there to help her if there's a problem, and we ask her to set the best time for the follow-up.

Figure 10-2 provides an example of the entry in the daily appointment schedule. "F:" means follow-up, and "SD" reminds me that the task was delegated to Sara Danvers.

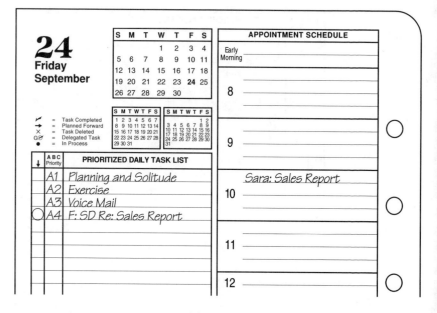

FIGURE 10-2
Follow-Up Symbol

Once you begin to follow this delegation process consistently, you will quickly develop a reputation as a project manager who follows through on details carefully. My assistant, Sandy Darlington, is one of the most talented people I have ever worked with. She has taught me a lot about delegation. She has refined the process so that I almost always get a progress report before the follow-up appointment time. She lets me know as soon as a delegated task has been completed.

This simple delegation process saves a lot of grief and worry. Under the old style of delegation, in the sales-report example above, we might have shown up at the meeting on Thursday assuming that the report would be ready, not knowing that a computer snafu had prevented it from being printed out. By finding out about the problem on Tuesday, we have time to figure out how to deal with it before the meeting.

Your greatest opportunity to follow up on delegated tasks,

however, comes from regularly scheduled project review meetings. You can save dozens of phone calls and stop-in visits by making this kind of follow-up a routine part of those meetings. Everyone who accepts a delegated task should know that this type of follow-up is a regular part of these meetings.

PROJECT REVIEW MEETINGS

Imagine this scene: You've just had a major surgical procedure, and the doctor rolls you out of the operating room and down to the hospital exit. He hands you a bunch of pills, orders you to rest for a few days, and tells you to have a nice life.

Ridiculous? Of course, but it's not far from what we do with projects. Often we develop a plan, hand out assignments, and go on our way, assuming the expected results will show up magically on the due date. Wrong!

Just as the doctor keeps the surgical patient in the hospital under close supervision for several days, monitoring vital signs, we have to monitor the vital signs of our projects. To do otherwise is malpractice. Perhaps the simplest method of monitoring projects is with regularly scheduled review meetings, yet when I ask project team members how often they have project review meetings, the most common answers are these: "What review meetings?" and "When we need them"— that is, when there's a problem. Sounds like a prescription for crisis management—not "Let's do everything we can to prevent problems," but rather "Let's wait till there's a problem, then figure out what to do about it."

The key to successful implementation of a project— assuming the visualization and planning steps were carried out effectively—is in project review meetings. With a carefully thought out and detailed plan in place, a review meeting is an opportunity to bring the entire team together, compare the plan to the actual experience, and discuss new information and changes. There are typically three items on the agenda for a review meeting:

1. What has happened so far?
2. What still needs to happen?
3. What problems, if any, are we having?

If this is done with key team members on a regular basis, problems can be prevented or resolved early on to keep the project on track. This is crucial for success. We will never be able to eliminate change and problems, but regular project review meetings can anticipate and avoid many problem situations. Throughout the implementation process, as changes and adjustments are made, it is important to update and revise the plan and the resources and to communicate the changes to everyone involved in the project.

On any given transcontinental flight, being off course by as little as a fraction of a percent would mean missing the target entirely, yet most flights are off course over 90 percent of the time! So why do almost all flights wind up at their intended destination? Because the pilots make continuous course corrections. By making frequent minor adjustments, they avoid making major corrections or missing the target altogether. Weekly project review meetings give you a chance to make minor course corrections and identify problems before they become disasters.

CREATING EFFECTIVE MEETINGS

Meetings are critical to organizational effectiveness. Meetings waste a great deal of time, reducing organizational effectiveness. Are both statements true?

Most people would consider meetings a necessary evil. The problem, however, isn't the meetings; it's the way most of them are managed. Most of us have suffered through so many boring, unproductive, time-wasting sessions that we shudder at the thought of another one. But meetings don't have to be boring and unproductive. They can provide a stimulating, challenging opportunity to share ideas and talents, to communicate new projects and information, and to make decisions.

To make meetings effective, we need to plan carefully and communicate the following information to all attendees:

- **Purpose and desired results:** Every meeting should have a purpose and specific desired results—to share new information, review a project, make a decision, schedule an event, create an action plan, or gain project approval, for example.
- **Attendees:** Invite only the people who can or will contribute or who will be affected by the outcome of the meeting. Try to avoid unnecessary political invitations; they only complicate and bog down the action.
- **Agenda:** Every meeting should have a written agenda to help people prepare information and ideas and to focus the meeting. Key questions to be addressed or decisions to be made should be included.
- **Time and place:** You need to specify the starting time, duration, and location of the meeting. Make sure the time and place suit the group and goals. Late afternoon meetings in hot, stuffy rooms are not conducive to new ideas and problem-solving.

COORDINATING MEETINGS WITH YOUR DAY PLANNER: THE MEETING PLANNER

Regardless of which day planner you're using, you will wind up customizing it to your specific needs, depending on the nature of your projects and the information and tasks you need to manage. Out of all the forms and processes discussed in this book, there may be only a few that are helpful to you.

The meeting form, however, is one I encourage all my workshop participants to use consistently, whether they are participants or facilitators. The reason for this is that the form helps guide a process that improves the content of a meeting, and it documents significant information from the meeting.

A meeting should not just be a single event that occurs at a specific time. Often the two most important elements of success are the preparation before and the follow-up after the meeting. The information entered on your meeting planner form will facilitate the preparation, the follow-up, and the actual discussion during the meeting. It gives you a guideline that you can use to make dramatic and immediate improvements in meeting efficiency. The magic is not in the form; it's in the process. The form simply guides you through the process. You can design your own customized form on a computer spreadsheet or a forms design program, or you can use the forms I use, which are available from Franklin Quest. Here's a description of each segment of the form I use:

Purpose and Desired Results

Just filling out these two lines on the meeting planner form ensures the clarification of meeting objectives prior to the meeting. The focus of the meeting will be much clearer after you identify this information. Consequently, it will be easier for you to keep the meeting on track. This information is vital to both the facilitator and the participants. If you are a participant but have not been informed of this information, it is appropriate to ask. After all, it is your time that is being requested for the meeting.

TIP—If you're a meeting facilitator and you can't complete these lines, you may want to cancel the meeting.

Meeting Planner

Date Scheduled
Meeting Title
Purpose
Desired Results
Location

Scheduled Time			Actual Time			Meeting Cost
Start	Stop	Total Hrs.	Siart	Stop	Total Hrs.	

Meeting Method		Meeting Type		
Facilitator		Recorder		
Group Leader		Time Keeper		
Group Members to Attend			Value Per Hr.	Total
1				
2				
3				
4				
5				
6				
7				
8				
9				

Items To Be Discussed	(Sequence)	#
1		
2		
3		
4		
5		
6		
7		
8		
9		
10		
11		
12		
13		
14		
15		
16		
17		
18		

CL 4022

FIGURE 10-3
Meeting Planner Form, Side One

Scheduled Time and Actual Time

Recording the scheduled time and actual time provides an ongoing reminder of the meeting culture within your organization. Do meetings typically start late and run overtime? If meetings start and end on time, it is because a standard has been set within an organization's culture. While it is hard to change the culture, it is possible to be a good role model and gradually change the expectations of the culture.

Meeting Method

This component answers the question, "How will this meeting be conducted?" A *directed discussion* meeting is directed by the use of an agenda, and participants are called on by a meeting leader, often to give reports pertaining to their items on the agenda. This format is typical of many staff meetings, weekly sales meetings, project meetings, and large committee meetings.

In an *open discussion* meeting, discussion is appropriate whenever attendees feel they have something significant to contribute. This method is common for quality control circles, small committee meetings, and other meetings of three to five people.

Meeting Type

By specifying the meeting type you answer the question, "What kind of meeting is this?" There are several types to choose from:

- Establishing goals and objectives
- Gathering information
- Planning
- Making decisions
- Coordinating
- Evaluating

Selecting the meeting type clarifies the purpose of the meeting. If you have ever left a meeting frustrated because no one made any decisions, perhaps you were in an information-gathering meeting rather than a decision-making meeting. Understanding the purpose of a meeting allows for better preparation and participation.

Meeting Roles

A common model for meetings has only two roles: the leader and the participants, and often the leader is also a participant. Several other roles are available within a meeting structure that can greatly improve meeting effectiveness. Here are some definitions and guidelines for these roles:

- **The facilitator** is not a participant in the meeting. The facilitator's role is to remain neutral, to control the progress of the meeting, and to guide it toward its objectives. This role is especially helpful when conflict resolution is a primary goal.
- **The recorder** has the responsibility of recording key information regarding distribution of agenda items, delegated tasks, and decisions reached.
- **The group leader** plans for and conducts the meeting to achieve the desired results. Often the group leader may fill other roles during the meeting if they are not assigned to someone else.
- **The time keeper** plays a vital role in keeping the meeting on schedule. This person is especially helpful when a group goes off on a tangent; the time keeper simply points out the time remaining on a particular item to help keep the topic from drifting. If time adjustments need to be made, the group leader can take appropriate action. The simple act of having a time keeper is a powerful key to successful meetings.

  When the Franklin Quest Planning for Results consultants (currently twenty-five of us) get together for our annual meeting, the only way we can get this group of talkative individuals through an agenda is with a time keeper. This function, along with a clear purpose and agenda, does more to foster success than anything else I have experienced. As the leader of the group, I choose the most time-conscious and assertive individual on the team to fill this role because sometimes it takes a somewhat bold individual to jump into the current conversation and remind participants of the time.

Group Members to Attend

This is simply a list of people who will attend the meeting. For a clear record I encourage you to put a check mark in the left column next to the names of the people who actually do attend. If you are the facilitator or leader, this will help you know who to share the information with later.

Value Per Hour and Total

Use this data to calculate meeting costs. Meetings can be an extremely costly use of resources. Sometimes a person who does not have signature authority to purchase $100 worth of supplies has the ability to call a meeting that may tie up thousands of dollars' worth of time. You may not complete this part of the form for every meeting, but I strongly recommend that every meeting facilitator or leader figure this out on occasion.

If you do not know the salary figures for the participants, call your human resources department. Tell them the type of job descriptions represented at that meeting. They can provide you with average figures without divulging confidential salary information.

Meetings are an investment that, by definition, should produce a return, and hopefully a good one. The return is difficult to measure, however, if we don't know how much we spent on the original investment. Use the information blocks to determine the direct hourly cost of the participant (salary plus benefits), the total for each participant according to the length of time of the meeting, and then add up the expense for the "meeting cost" block on the form.

As you begin thinking about calling a meeting to solve a problem, consider these questions: Is it worth it? Can your meeting provide an adequate return on investment? This information should help you look more critically at your meeting, especially in terms of scheduled time versus actual time. This is the best motivation I have ever seen to encourage organizations to create a culture of on-time meetings. Add up what it costs to wait fifteen minutes for a key participant. You will never want it to happen again.

Items to Be Discussed

Create your agenda on this portion of the form. By using this page in your day planner you can gather ideas as they occur and not leave the preparation until the last moment.

As soon as you learn of a meeting, take out a blank meeting planner form (I keep several blank forms behind a tab in my day planner). Fill out any information you have at the time— date, time, location, and so on—and place the form in your day planner on the dated page for the day of the meeting. In other words, if today is June 7 and the meeting is in two weeks, on June 21, place the form so it will appear in your day planner on June 21. You never know where you might be or what you might be doing when you think of items to discuss at the meeting. You could be in another meeting, talking on the phone, working at your desk, shopping at the grocery store, or taking a shower when you think of something to add to the agenda. All you do is open your day planner to that page (the monthly calendar will direct you to the correct page, because of course you wrote the meeting on that calendar) and add the agenda item to the list. (Hopefully you're out of the shower and somewhat dry by this time!) Then, just before the meeting, as you do your preparation, you can sequence the items if necessary, provide a time frame for each item, and your meeting preparation is done.

Distributing the agenda to the other participants before the meeting helps them prepare for the meeting, and you may even get additional agenda suggestions from them.

Material and Preparation Needed

In this section (see Figure 10-1), list the items needed at the meeting including flip chart, pens, overhead projector, and so forth. This also gives you an opportunity to be clear about whose responsibility it is to bring each one.

The portions of the form discussed above were all used for meeting preparation. The remaining parts are used during the actual meeting.

Delegated Tasks

Use this section to record notes about tasks that are delegated and to whom. If an item is delegated to you, make sure you give that item an asterisk and put it in your project task map or daily task list with enough time to complete the task.

Meeting Notes

Record here the important highlights, decisions, and discussions raised throughout the meeting. If you run out of space, just insert a blank daily record-of-events page behind this form, title it "Meeting Notes, cont'd," and continue as long as necessary. Because you are recording only the highlights, you won't run out of space very often.

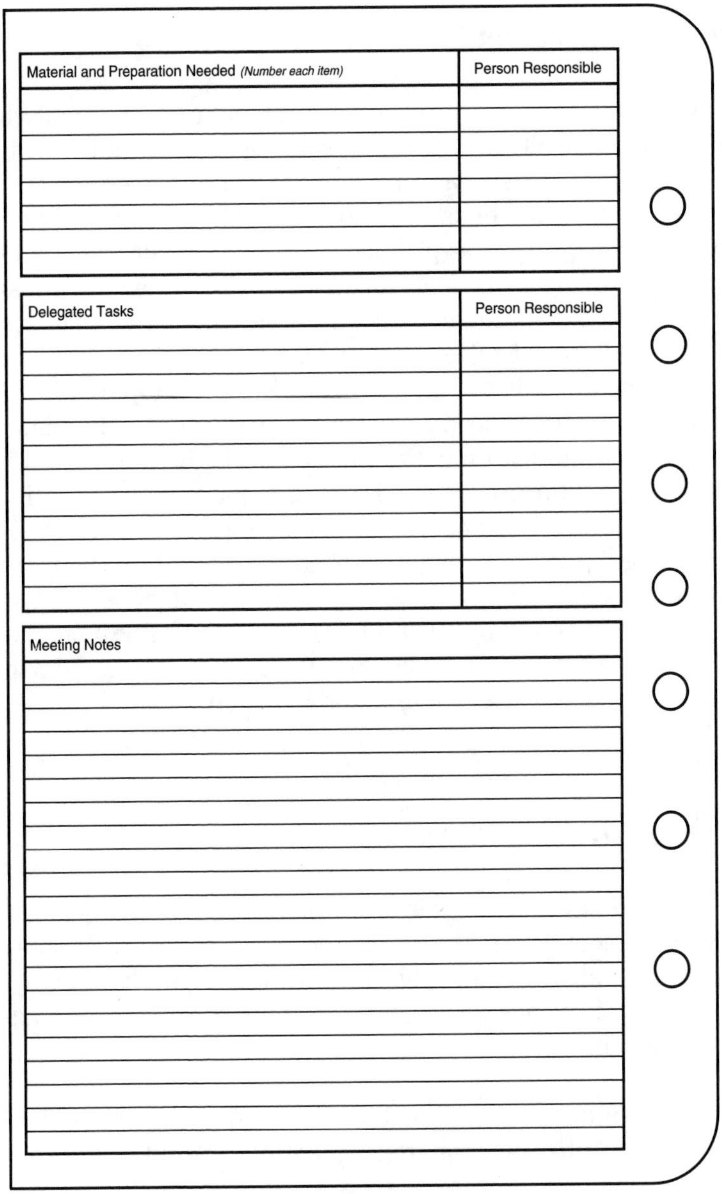

Material and Preparation Needed *(Number each item)*	Person Responsible

Delegated Tasks	Person Responsible

Meeting Notes

FIGURE 10-4
Meeting Planner Form, Side Two

TULE MEETINGS

One specific type of project review meeting is particularly helpful, especially near the end of a project. It is a meeting to Tie Up Loose Ends, or a TULE meeting (pronounced too-lee). Projects and loose ends seem to go hand in hand. Regardless of how well a project is planned, neglected details eventually start surfacing. As you get further into the project, you may want to add a TULE discussion to the agenda of regularly scheduled project review meetings.

Mindmapping is a helpful process for TULE topics. Simply write the words "Loose Ends" in the center of the mindmap and lead a brainstorming discussion with the team. This is when the Editor in our mind is doing its job very well. It's that little voice that pops up every once in a while and says, "Uh-oh. I wonder who's taking care of that?" Map those thoughts. During the brainstorming process, maybe someone will say, "Oh, don't worry about that; I have it covered." But if it is not covered, the team can now specify, right on the mindmap, who is going to take care of it and by when.

MEETING ATTENDANCE

If you are new in your role and working on a recently established project, you may find that perfect attendance at meetings is a challenge. Since this is a new project, perhaps no one is taking it seriously yet. Here are four ways to encourage attendance:

1. During the kickoff meeting involve the team in the decision as to how often these meetings should be held and when.
2. Assure the team—again, at the kickoff meeting—that each meeting will be brief and will have a clear agenda.

The purpose of the meeting will be to review the plan, review each person's progress, and make any necessary changes or adjustments. Attendance at every meeting will be vital for team members to understand the plan and the dynamics of the project.

3. Before the meeting, distribute copies of the meeting planner form to each participant as a reminder of the meeting date, time, place, agenda, and other information. You can place this reminder on the daily page of all team members' day planners to ensure that they receive it and so that you won't hear the old standby, "No one told me about the meeting."

4. If any team members miss a meeting, call them immediately after the meeting to make sure they are okay. Let them know they were greatly missed and then ask them for the progress report they would have given you at the meeting. They will quickly understand that meetings are to be taken seriously and that their participation is important.

Team members will soon come to understand that the information shared during the meeting is vital to their understanding of their individual parts and of the project as a whole. When the project manager makes an effort to keep the meeting positive in tone and full of information and creative problem-solving techniques, he or she won't have to do much else to encourage attendance. Participants will not want to miss the information provided. Remember, keep the meetings brief and to the point.

MEETINGS AND RELATIONSHIPS

Meetings are a time when relationships can be nurtured through face-to-face contact. In our present world of e-mail and voice mail, we may use those tools almost exclusively, forgetting that success is attained by people who believe in a project and make it a success. Electronic communication should be an aid to communication, not a substitute for building relationships.

In today's matrix-style organizations, project managers often do not have direct responsibility for staff members who serve on project teams. Positive, information-sharing meetings can help build relationships that are vital to the success of such projects. These meetings can be creative sessions in which people can explore ideas and information. Contributors should feel that their participation is welcomed, and they should know that the project manager is there as a coach, willing to help team members whenever needed.

Communicating and coordinating projects with other people is a critical project management skill. However, the increasing complexity of today's projects requires collaboration across a broad expanse of functions, locations, time shifts, and responsibility levels. Most projects are not done by officially designated teams; they are done as informal collaborations. The next chapter will help you understand how to have more productive collaborations.

CHAPTER 11

IMPLEMENT

Creative Collaboration

COMING ATTRACTIONS:
- Barriers to collaboration
- Collaboration enhancers
- Collaboration rooms
- What's your CQ?

Nothing new that is really interesting comes without collaboration.

—JAMES WATSON

One log doesn't make a fire, and most teamwork doesn't happen on teams.

In today's complex, interdependent society, few things happen as the result of only one person's efforts. Teamwork is a fundamental requirement for all organizations, yet most teamwork doesn't happen on formal, organized teams. A lot of what we call teamwork is really something else.

Most of us find ourselves working on projects with other people who are not formally connected to us, people we have no authority over, people who may benefit only indirectly from the outcome of the project, people who may already have a full complement of their own projects. We may work with one group of people on one project and a completely different group on another project. There may be no formal team leader, no recognized team goals, no team facilitator or coach, no celebration of the team when a project is completed—because there is no "team." So what is this thing we're doing when we marshal the resources of a diverse group of people to accomplish an objective? The term that describes it best is "creative collaboration."

Creative collaboration is the effort to create a result that requires the *creative contributions* of two or more persons. Creative collaboration is not the same as one person having responsibility for a project and simply delegating tasks to other people. In a creative collaboration, there is shared responsibility, a co-creation of the project design and expected results, a give-and-take that enhances and builds beyond the original vision. This sounds like something rather magical and uncontrollable . . . and it is. But while it may not be controllable in the strict sense of the word, creative collaboration can be nurtured and encouraged.

Surprisingly enough, it's based on only a few simple principles. These principles enhance the results of formal teamwork as well as informal collaborations. Before we discuss the principles that nurture collaboration, however, it's important to understand the organizational barriers that often block collaboration.

BARRIERS TO COLLABORATION

Collaboration is not something that has to be forced; it's a natural phenomenon, a result of the human condition, unless it is blocked. A fictional example of collaboration is Radar, the grape-soda-sucking supply corporal from the television series *M*A*S*H*. Radar demonstrates the power of creative collaboration. Acting in a position of little authority and going completely outside the official policies and procedures of his organization, Radar collaborates with his peers in other camps to reassign supplies. The results, while often bizarre, are almost always more efficient than the planned allocation by military headquarters. Radar may be a fictional character, but most organizations benefit from a high level of covert, underground collaboration and bartering.

There are two very effective ways to block collaboration: by obstructing the flow of information and by impeding interaction between members of the organization. Anything that restricts the sharing of information or interpersonal interactions will hamper collaboration. Common organizational barriers include:

- Need-to-know policies
- Rigid hierarchies
- Chain-of-command communication restrictions
- Lack of easily accessible meeting spaces
- Narrow job definitions
- Separation of functional areas
- Focus on individual or departmental objectives
- Compensation policies focused only on individual incentives
- Lack of social meeting places such as coffee rooms, cafeterias, and gyms
- Shiftwork
- Policies governing wall space usage
- Lack of communication technology such as voice mail and e-mail

Collaboration occurs in spite of barriers. What would happen if we removed the barriers to creative collaboration? This actually happened at Marshall Industries, an electronics distributor with approximately a billion dollars in sales per year. Marshall had learned the lessons of management by objectives and had rigorously developed meaningful personal objectives for almost every employee in the organization. When CEO Rob Rodin learned about organizational systems from quality guru W. Edwards Deming, he started looking more closely at

Marshall and discovered a set of distortions common to most organizations. In order to meet numerical goals, employees of most organizations routinely:

- Ship ahead of schedule
- Argue heatedly over expense allocations
- Distort budget requirements
- Hold customer returns or credits
- Accept bad business
- Fudge reports
- Establish territories and compete internally
- Place internal politics ahead of customer needs
- Experience a month-end panic and rush to ship, sell, or produce
- Make short-term decisions
- Manipulate inventory levels

Under Rodin's direction, Marshall Industries found a way to stop that insanity, but their new method shattered the fundamental beliefs of their industry and of business in general. Over half of the Marshall employees are salespeople, and the company deals with over 140 manufacturers who want the salespeople to sell their products. On top of the normal sales commissions system, a complex and often conflicting array of vendor-promoted sales incentives and contests had developed. When Marshall's leaders realized that this system had created barriers to people working together, they gradually eliminated all sales commissions, incentives, and contests and all management-by-objective compensation programs.

This action shook the foundation of the electronic component distribution industry. Responses ranged from "It's about time!" to "This is communism!" Business and industry media jumped on the story and debated the decision in articles and letters. Management theorists claimed that Marshall didn't understand incentive systems or the motivation of salespeople, while industry analysts predicted a loss of customers, suppliers, and top salespeople.

What actually happened, however, was that some of the barriers to collaboration were removed, and results were dramatic: annual sales soared from $600 million to over $1 billion, profits doubled, the stock price tripled, individual productivity doubled, and not one top salesperson left the company, in spite of a few large drops in individual compensation.

Marshall's approach to compensation may not be the answer for every organization, but it does show the power of removing organizational obstacles to collaboration. At Marshall this barrier was a crazy-quilt system of individual incentives, contests, and promotions. Other organizations may have completely different obstacles preventing people from collaborating on a shared vision.

THE COLLABORATION CHICKEN-AND-EGG

In order for people to collaborate together, there must be a project, a challenge, or an opportunity to work on. Like a project, a collaboration is a temporary activity. It has an objective or goal, and once that is achieved, the collaboration is finished. If a problem or challenge is of genuine interest to the organization, the information that a project to address it exists, or is being contemplated, will generally attract collaborators. Additionally, if an environment encourages and supports frequent interaction, people will begin to talk about problems and challenges, which will lead to decisions to collaborate on those projects. So which comes first, the project or the collaborators? It doesn't matter. What's really important is that the environment is information-rich and interaction-rich. If those two elements exist, the projects and collaborators will find each other.

COLLABORATION ENHANCERS

In an environment that is information- and interaction-rich, five basic principles will naturally stimulate and enhance collaboration:

1. **Relationships.** Relationships are the foundation of collaboration. To have a healthy foundation, an environment should be one of mutual trust and respect, shared values and commitment, and appropriate recognition and rewards.
2. **Shared values.** This relates not only to individual and organizational values such as honesty and customer service but to group values as well. Jay Elggren, a Franklin Quest trainer, works with teams in the aerospace industry, to help them develop their own team Productivity Pyramid (see Chapter 3). If, for example, a team identifies effective team communication as a value, they can develop objectives for improving communication practices. Identifying "effective project documentation" as a value helped one team define ways to improve overall data collection techniques. These written values, created and defined by the team members, helped create a buy-in on the part of all of the team members and improve overall project performance.
3. **Shared vision.** Collaboration does not eliminate conflict. Anytime more than one person is involved with a project, there will be disagreements and differences. However, if the collaborators share the same vision, they will find ways to resolve differences or design acceptable compromises in order to continue on the path to the shared vision. The passion and enthusiasm that come from a shared vision provide the energy needed to work through the rough spots and conflicts.
4. **Shared creative space.** Collaborators need a space in which to co-create. This can be as simple as an available

whiteboard or large sheets of paper on a wall or a shared computer system or network. Or it can be a more formal, specially adapted meeting room. The space has to invite, encourage, and even demand the participation of all of the collaborators. Shared creative space makes it easier for people to organize and interact with information and with each other.

5. **Fun.** Perhaps the number one clue that creative collaboration is happening is laughter. Laughter and fun free the mind from barriers and restrictions.

⌘ ***Ponder Point:*** *The average desk is a work space for one. It does not invite—or even tolerate, in most cases—collaboration. What would a collaborative work space look like?*

COLLABORATIVE TOOLS

Collaborative tools make it easier for people to co-create. They make it easy for everyone involved to participate. They make information visual and movable so as to facilitate new connections and links.

Just as a whiteboard invites collaboration while an overhead projector doesn't, some tools are collaborative and some aren't. One of the most powerful collaboration tools is mindmapping. In addition to being an effective way to think about values, brainstorm ideas, and break projects into pieces, mindmapping is also a terrific collaboration tool. Collaborative mindmapping works just like individual mindmapping, although there is an important consideration when mindmapping in a group—group conformity pressures.

Diversity is a prerequisite for good collaboration and brainstorming. However, diversity generally means varying levels of expertise as well as different levels of authority and power. Too often the person with the highest level of perceived expertise or authority leads the group, intentionally or unintentionally, down the path of his or her own thinking. The expert or boss says, "We could do x," and people start thinking, "Yeah, x is a good idea. Maybe x plus one would be nice." They focus on x and don't even consider a or m or dlb.

Preventing this natural tendency to move in the direction of the recognized leader will require a special effort to level the playing field. The novice must somehow be made to feel as comfortable as the senior expert, because often the best ideas come from the person who knows little about the problem but has experience in another field that can be adapted to the current situation. Unless that person speaks up and is heard, that winning idea may never surface.

Here are two ways to counteract group conformity pressures:

1. **Anonymity.** Allow participants to submit unattributed ideas. Ideas can be written on sticky notes or index cards, or they can be input into computer systems combined with specialized software that collects the ideas and projects them onto a screen for further idea stimulation, editing, and evaluation.
2. **Individual thinking time.** Some people think and speak their ideas rapidly while others need time to reflect and develop their ideas. If there is going to be an open brainstorming session, begin with a short individual session where individuals mindmap their ideas or write them on sticky notes. This gives everyone a chance to formulate their ideas and lessens the likelihood that everyone will start down one path and not consider others.

All group brainstorming and collaboration efforts depend on energy management techniques. The more energy a group develops for a topic, the more ideas they will generate. Here are a few ways to stimulate group energy when mindmapping or using any other collaborative tool:

- **Size of mindmapping space.** The larger the space, the more ideas will be generated. A void is created that stimulates an urge to fill it. Some collaboration rooms now have an entire wall of whiteboard. You can also tape sheets of easel paper together to form a "thinking wall."
- **Scribe or no scribe.** Most groups opt to have one person act as the scribe to collect the ideas as they are presented. This is a critical position; this person needs to capture *all* ideas as presented with a minimum of editing. In a fast-moving session, it's almost impossible for one person to handle the flow of ideas.

  Other groups choose to let each person write his or her own ideas. This method almost always generates more energy and participation. However, it's important for all members to say their ideas as well as write them down, so everyone else in the group hears each idea. This will help others make connections and formulate their own ideas. Encourage people to branch off of other people's ideas. If everyone uses a different color pen, the map will take on a wild, colorful look, and you can actually see how ideas bounce around and stimulate each other.
- **Brainstorming rules.** Reinforce the standard rules of brainstorming: no judgments, quantity wanted, wild ideas accepted, and bouncing off other ideas encouraged. A study done by Arthur VanGundy, a communications professor at the University of Oklahoma, showed that a group that had these rules reinforced generated twice as many ideas as a group that did not have this reminder.
- **Standing or sitting.** More energy and ideas are generated when the group stands than if the participants are seated.
- **Different perspectives.** Rotate the mindmap occasionally, change seats, or move to a new room to give everyone a different perspective.
- **Killer balls.** Judgment (good or bad) and lengthy discussion are fatal to idea generation. To halt judgmental comments and long-winded definitions or defenses, try

using killer balls. These are soft foam balls available in toy departments. Give all members of the group a killer ball and tell them to throw them at anyone who utters a killer phrase—"We tried that once," or "would cost too much," or "against policy"—and at anyone who goes on for more than thirty seconds. Have participants practice throwing the balls at each other a couple of times to get the feel of it.

- **Sticky-mapping.** One disadvantage of standard mind-mapping is that the information is not movable. You can avoid this flaw by having members write their ideas and information on sticky notes. Each person can brainstorm individually, writing one idea on each note. Then all the notes can be placed on the map, with related ideas clumped together. Notes can then be rearranged, duplicates eliminated, and new ideas added until the group is satisfied with the map.

- **Computer mapping.** Group mindmapping can also be done with the assistance of a software program called Inspiration. Using a projection system, members of the group can call out ideas and see them captured on the screen, using a function known as "rapid-fire." Participants can then arrange, connect, and edit the ideas and put them into a graphically pleasing format for distribution to members of the group and to other interested parties.

ALL COLLABORATIVE TOOLS MUST BE _____

- **Participative.** The tool draws people into the process.
- **Visual.** Information is presented so that the entire group can see it.
- **Movable.** Information and ideas are easily rearranged, grouped, combined, and edited.
- **Fun.** The tool stimulates wildness and a relaxed sense of humor and fun.

The book *Transformation Thinking* by Joyce Wycoff and Tim Richardson provides more information about other collaborative tools such as brainwriting, mess mapping, story-boarding, fishboning, and mindscaping.

MEETING ROOMS AND COLLABORATION ROOMS

Most meeting and conference rooms are designed for presentations, not collaboration. The standard setup is a long conference table surrounded by chairs, perhaps a whiteboard, an overhead projector, and a video system. These rooms are designed primarily for information presentation. One person sits or stands at the front of the room and presents information, using the whiteboard, the overhead projector, or the video monitor. Participants are focused on the front of the room and the information being presented. Discussion may or may not be encouraged, but participants are seldom invited to take control of the pen or the overhead or monitor. There is no real co-creation of information and understanding.

Now imagine instead a different type of room—a collaboration room. This room is surrounded with floor-to-ceiling whiteboards. There are flip charts supplied with sticky notes that can be posted on the whiteboards. The room is well supplied with colored pens as well as Post-It notes of various sizes and colors that can be used for brainstorming and storyboarding on the whiteboards.

Tables and chairs are smaller, allowing room to stand up, walk around, and gather in groups. The room has a phone and a computer system complete with creativity and organizational software and connection to the internal and external e-mail system and a printer. There is a copy machine in the room or close by.

TIP—If you want people to use creativity and organizational software, make it easy for them to learn how to use it. Put tutorials or training videos in the collaboration room.

⌘ **Ponder Point:** *The American Society for Training and Development (ASTD) states that American companies are spending only 1.4 percent of their payroll on training. Japanese- and European-owned companies based in the United States spend three to five times more on employee training than American-owned companies. The ASTD study also points out that training reaches only about 10 percent of the workforce. What does that say to and about the other 90 percent?*

This collaboration room is organized to stimulate conversation and interaction. It's easy for people to grab a pen and begin to mindmap or sketch a model on the wall. They can instantly access information from sources outside the room via the phone, the e-mail system, or the unlimited number of information databases accessible by modem.

This is a low-tech version of a collaboration room that could be developed by almost any organization. Even more sophisticated versions are being developed by Xerox, GM, IBM, Apple, EDS, and dozens of other corporations. These rooms are generally equipped with computer stations for attendees and specialized, sophisticated software to facilitate brainstorming and idea manipulation.

In a study cited by Michael Schrage in *No More Teams, Mastering the Dynamics of Creative Collaboration,* IBM asserts that these "Decision Support Centers" generate over 50 percent in person-hour savings in meeting time and a 92 percent reduction in time required to complete a project. While these high-tech collaboration rooms are wonderful, a great deal of the collaborative benefit can be gained by simply using the available resources.

"I could see myself being heard."

Bernard DeKoven, author of *Connected Executives* and a pioneer of the collaborative meeting concept, advocates a relatively low-tech approach because it is accessible to anyone. In his meetings, he uses a computer and projection system with standard software and a "technographer," a person who facilitates participation, communication, and buy-in through the artful use of the system. By using software that people in the organization are already familiar with, he reduces learning time and makes people more aware of the benefit of collaboration and less likely to think that the software is the magic. This process turns standard word processing, outlining, or spreadsheet software into "groupware."

In DeKoven's process, the technographer (the person operating the computer system) enters information as it is generated by the group. DeKoven describes the process of planning sessions as the "C-cycle," consisting of three parts—collecting information and ideas, connecting them, and correcting them.

In one recent example, DeKoven worked with a hotel in a bottom-up planning process. All of the front-line hotel employees were brought into sessions of seventy-five to one hundred people at a time and asked to brainstorm all of the things that would make the hotel better. As they made suggestions, the technographer entered them into the system and they were projected on a huge screen so that everyone could see them at once. This group, consisting of maids, desk clerks, bellmen, room service waiters, and other employees, was not accustomed to being involved in this type of process and being listened to. One person remarked in some amazement, "I could see myself being heard."

The next part of the process was to bring in mid-level managers and have them continue building on the ideas generated by the first group. Using the same process, they arranged, rearranged, connected, and disconnected ideas until they had categorized ideas into five themes for improvement.

This information was turned over to senior-level managers to have them develop solutions for each theme. At the end of this part of this session, a printout of the report was made and copies were made for every member of the group. A celebration was held, the reports were passed out, and people were invited to sign each other's copies. Not only was this an extremely effective problem-solving process but it generated an almost 100 percent buy-in from the people who would be responsible for implementing the solutions.

WHAT'S YOUR ORGANIZATION'S CQ (COLLABORATIVE QUOTIENT)?

The following evaluation will help you determine how well your organization supports collaboration. Rate your organization from 1 to 5 on the following questions.

1. Terrible/never
2. Poor/seldom
3. Average/generally
4. Good/often
5. Excellent/always

___ 1. We stimulate communication by providing conference rooms, whiteboards, bulletin boards, open work areas.

___ 2. We share information widely through group meetings, newsletters, e-mail, closed-circuit TV, financial and performance reports.

___ 3. We have a high level of trust and respect for each other.

___ 4. We encourage people to collaborate on projects and allow them to identify potential projects even when it takes time away from normal duties.

___ 5. We have a compensation policy that rewards collaborative efforts as well as individual efforts.

___ 6. Our organization's values, vision, and objectives are clearly understood by all, and we encourage groups and individuals to clarify their own values and vision.

__ 7. Rewards and risks are shared equitably by everyone in the organization.

__ 8. We have computer-enhanced collaboration tools and groupware in place, and everyone in the organization has access to these tools.

__ 9. We encourage informal interaction across departments and functions and have an "open access" policy for everyone in the organization.

__10. Most of the time, most of our people take pride in their work and frequently talk about work being fun.

SCORES

50	**Congratulations!** Check your perceptions with the first five people you meet. If they rate these questions the same way you do, call us. We would like to hear your story!
45–49	Yours is a rare organization. Somehow you've managed to do what everyone else is talking about doing. Keep up the good work!
40–44	You're on the right track, but you need to open your lines of communication. Ask people (all people) what would make their work life better? What tools do they need? What information do they need? Do they understand the work processes and how they fit into the whole?
39 or less	Organize a collaboration group to discuss ways to stimulate collaboration—before it's too late.

Collaboration is a critical part of project completion and depends greatly on your ability to coordinate and communicate the project vision and the plan for achieving it to everyone involved with the project. It requires the ability to recognize potential hazards and create backup plans that can be implemented when the inevitable glitch occurs.

However, once the project objective has been reached, the

project is not over. It is important to know how to close the project, evaluate the lessons learned that can be applied to future projects, and celebrate its success. The next chapter will give you some important information about this often neglected step.

CHAPTER 12

CLOSE

The Foundation for Future Success

C O M I N G   A T T R A C T I O N S :
- Project evaluation
- Documentation
- Project priorities matrix

---

*You can't build a reputation
on what you're* going *to do.*

—HENRY FORD

Every project is a learning experience. Think about how many projects you will have managed one year from now ... five years or ten years from now. If we learn from each one, our expertise will grow with each project.

Almost every project has elements that we liked and would want to repeat as well as elements we did not like and would not want to repeat. Looking at the highlights and the lowlights of a project is a critical part of the learning process. Unfortunately, it is often overlooked in the rush to get on with other things, even though it's one of the activities that separates the expert from the average project manager. This chapter shows you how to look at the lessons to be learned from a completed project.

An easy way to start a project review is with a simple questionnaire such as the ones on the following pages. These can be used by an individual or a team. If there was a project team, try to get each member to complete the questionnaire. Since each member has a different perspective, it's important to get a complete view.

PROJECT EVALUATION

Project Title: _____

Project Manager: _____

Project Start Date: _____ Completion Date: _____

Did the project meet budget specifications?	Y	N
Did the project meet time line specifications?	Y	N
Did the project meet technical (quality) specifications?	Y	N

Rank each question: 1 = lowest performance

5 = highest performance

Did end results meet original expected results?	1 2 3 4 5
How well did I (we) accomplish what was actually achievable?	1 2 3 4 5
How achievable (realistic) was the original plan?	1 2 3 4 5
How do others view the success of the project?	1 2 3 4 5
Customer	1 2 3 4 5
Team members	1 2 3 4 5
Management	1 2 3 4 5
Self	1 2 3 4 5
Others _____	1 2 3 4 5
How well did I (we) implement the plan?	1 2 3 4 5
How well did I (we) revise and update the plan when needed?	1 2 3 4 5
Were necessary resources available?	1 2 3 4 5
Were review meetings timely?	1 2 3 4 5
Were review meetings managed effectively?	1 2 3 4 5
Was project documentation adequate?	1 2 3 4 5

PROJECT PROBLEM ANALYSIS

Think of some of the rough spots on this project and suggest ways that they could have been fixed or avoided. Or document some of the primary problems encountered on this project. Describe the problem and explain how it was solved.

Problem description: _____

_____

_____

Solution suggestions: _____

_____

_____

Problem description: _____

_____

_____

Solution suggestions: _____

_____

_____

Project highlights and accomplishments: _____

_____

_____

What would you do differently next time? _____

_____

_____

_____

The information from the project-evaluation questionnaire can provide valuable information about what worked well and might be applied to the next project, and what did not work well and should be avoided on the next project.

DOCUMENTATION

Closing out and filing project documentation is an important activity that can help officially close down a project. This can be one of the trickiest stages of all, however, because projects tend to linger at this stage. Perhaps the bulk of the project has been completed, the pressure is off, and the project is unofficially considered done, but there are still loose ends that need to be tied up.

At this point, you should remove any remaining project files from your planner and store them in your desk project management notebook. Label the file tab with the name of the project. It is helpful to keep a table of contents in the front of the notebook to clearly list project titles and other important information. This can also be used to track other related project files and where they are stored—most commonly in folders in the "Completed Projects" section of your file system. There should be only a few places to look for project information. Source documents are typically located in clearly labeled file folders, and the information that helped you manage the project is located in your project management notebook.

The importance of documentation varies with the job. For many projects, documentation is simply helpful information to have access to for future modifications, to use in managing similar projects in the future, or to assist in the evaluation process. For other projects, however, it is much more than that. Detailed project documentation may be required by law. Future maintenance on new products or programs may depend on careful documentation created during development.

1996 Project Index

Project Title:	Description:	Start Date:	Completion Date:	Other Related Files:
<u>Client Project</u>	Improve client customization services	January '96	March '96	Computer Files: CLIENT.DOC CLPROJ.INS
<u>Book Illustrations</u>	Illustrations and artwork for new book	May '96	June '96	Computer Files: Zip disk: Form Files Zip disk: Book Art TOFCONT.XLS Notebook Files: Book Illustrations Book: Rough Draft
<u>Training Program</u>	Custom train-the-train-er program for ABC Corp.	August '96	October '96	Completed Projects File: XYZ Corp. Computer Files: MANUAL.DOC

FIGURE 12-1
Project Index—In Front of Notebook

The contents of your project documentation will depend on the nature of your project, the environment, and the requirements. It is important to have a consistent system so that each completed project has the necessary documentation stored the same way. The goal is complete data and information and an effective retrieval system.

If the project files are large, it is helpful to include subdivider tabs within a project file. Sometimes top-cut tabs are helpful for this purpose.

WHAT'S NEXT?

As we near the completion of a project, we usually have already started to think about our next projects—or other people are starting to think about us for their projects. If we

FIGURE 12-2
Project Notebook with Top-Cut Tabs

have successfully completed our current projects, possibilities for new projects are generally abundant. Prioritizing multiple projects is one of the greatest challenges we face. There should be a T-shirt that reads "So many projects . . . so little time." There will always be too much to do. It's easy to become tyrannized by our own success if we just keep stacking the priorities deeper and deeper, treating them all as if they are all so important that they must be done right now. Prioritizing multiple projects is a skill that has become vital during these "hurry, do more, and do it faster" times. A fast, simple, and powerful technique to help you prioritize projects is the *project priorities matrix*.

PROJECT PRIORITIES MATRIX

This technique builds on the A-B-C prioritizing technique described in Chapter 4. We have expanded the model to add a few important dimensions.

We have added D for worthless projects, for example. It is helpful sometimes to acknowledge that certain projects on our wish list are actually pretty low on the totem pole in terms of worth. These we can safely put aside for quite some time— perhaps indefinitely. My son used to put cleaning his room in this category. Well, one person's priority may not be another's. Of course, in this case, peace and harmony in the home required compromise on both our parts.

Second, we have added the "future" dimension. Some projects may become extremely important at a later date, but we can safely put them on the back burner for now. To accurately place each project in its proper box within the matrix requires a careful look at the concept of "return on investment" (ROI).

A project exists because a payoff can be expected when the project is successfully completed. These payoffs are tied directly to our values and our long-range goals. It is helpful to keep these values and goals in mind as we evaluate the

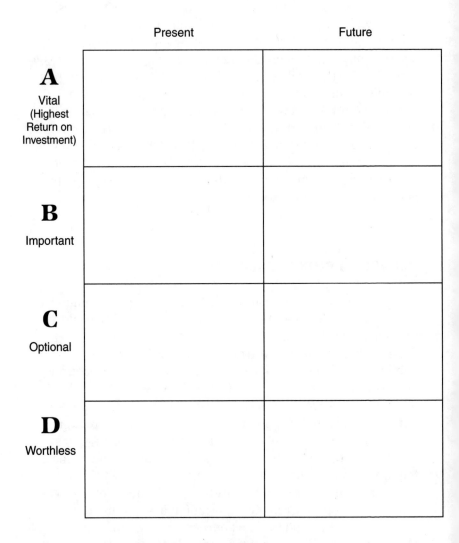

FIGURE 12-3
Project Priorities Matrix

project's overall importance, in terms of the value of the result netted by the completion of the project.

The overall value netted by the result of the project is the project's return on investment. Using that criterion, you can compare projects to one another to determine where the highest return on investment is found.

An excellent way to prioritize value among projects is to put the project priorities matrix on a flip chart or whiteboard and write the projects on sticky notes. Place each note in the appropriate box on the matrix, based on the project's ROI. The sticky notes allow easy moving and reevaluation. This is important, because on the first pass you'll almost always put all projects in the A-Present box.

I learned to use this technique near the end of my first year as director of public seminars for Franklin Quest (now Franklin Covey). By then I was swamped with projects and feeling slightly out of control. My boss at the time was Dick Winwood, one of the founders of Franklin. I walked into his office one day and asked him to help me prioritize my projects. He was delighted that I had asked for his help. I drew the matrix on a flip chart, and one by one I posted the notes in the boxes where Dick thought they should go. Of course, every yellow sticky landed in the A-Present box. Finally Dick looked at the matrix, then at me, and said, "I see your point. Maybe we'd better rethink some of these."

We looked very carefully at each project and compared it to the other projects. We moved a few projects to the B-Present box, as we realized that they were important but not vital. We even found one C and one that we could slip to the A-Future box. That decision was most valuable to me, because it was a large project that had been competing for my time and attention. It was a great relief to realize that it was vital but that it could wait until the A-Present projects were done.

This exercise provided me with a clear understanding of my highest priorities over the next several months. Now I use this tool in my department strategic planning on a quarterly basis. We have a fiscal year business plan that clarifies the values, goals, and projects for the department for a year.

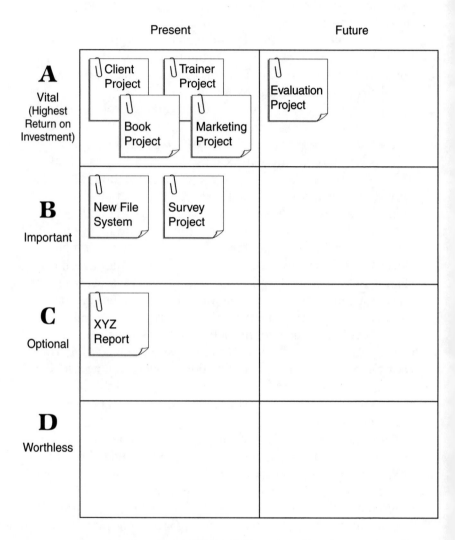

FIGURE 12-4
Example: Project Priorities Matrix

These projects are arranged on the project priorities matrix ninety days at a time. This way, the department staff can clearly see the most important projects to focus on. Ninety days later, we check off the projects that have been completed, and rearrange the priorities for the next ninety days. Now, some of the projects that had been A-Future become A-Present. Some of the B's may become A's. Surprisingly enough, however, some of the B's may become C's, or drop off into the D box.

Not every idea for a project is necessarily a good one. An idea may sound good at the time when it's presented. But later, with more information, it may not seem relevant or timely. It is very helpful to evaluate a project idea over time, with the advantage of a gestation period.

As new project suggestions or assignments come in, they can be evaluated along with the other projects and assigned a place on the matrix. In some departments and companies, work assignments may come in and affect the current assignments. This technique provides a helpful way to evaluate these new assignments compared to the existing projects. A new assignment is given a rating on the matrix so it can be scheduled into the work flow in the most timely way.

CELEBRATE

Finally it is celebration time. Don't miss the opportunity to throw a celebration and acknowledge everyone's participation with a show of appreciation and thanks. While a project may end, often the relationships that were developed during the project do not. Future projects often involve the same people. Team synergy is a function of relationships. As time goes by, many project managers connect with a group of people who become a core group for future projects.

Celebrations can be as simple as a wrap-up meeting with refreshments or as elaborate as an off-site resort getaway. If possible, find a way to let people sign the project to show their participation. If the project was a small piece of a bigger project, let people see how their efforts fit into the whole. Give people a chance to meet and talk with the project's customers. Celebration should be about building pride, making people feel good about their contribution to the project.

Also, celebrating the successful completion of a project is an important acknowledgment of project closure and the passage to new projects. A project is different from a process or other routine work because it has an end. It is important to formally acknowledge that ending.

A FINAL NOTE FROM THE AUTHORS

The first project you can celebrate is the completion of this book. We hope you will benefit from the project completion process outlined here. It has changed both of our lives, allowing us to be more effective and achieve dreams we never thought possible. We encourage you to try the techniques described in the previous chapters. Try them, play with them, and adapt them to your particular needs. This is a starting point. You will probably find some of the ideas far more useful to you than others. Use them and know that the others are always here if you need to come back to them.

And don't worry about doing any of this perfectly. After Joyce implemented the desk system discussed in Chapter 5, for instance, it worked for her for about six months. Then a major project claimed all of her attention and she lost control of her desk for several months. Once the storm was over, however, she was able to catch up and reimplement the system.

The project management processes discussed here are not about perfection. They're about making progress, learning better ways to choose projects based on our values, and effectively completing those chosen projects. After you complete a project, review the process you used to manage and complete it. If there are areas where you think you might have been more effective, go back to that section of the book and review the process discussed there. After a few projects, the process will become automatic and you will have become an expert project completer.

Good luck and may all your projects be joyful!

FORMS TO HELP YOU GET STARTED

If you do not want to make your own forms, you can purchase project forms directly from Franklin Covey or request a catalog by calling (800) 654-1776. Forms are available in three sizes:

Monarch: 8½" by 11", 7-hole format
Classic: 5½" by 8½", 7-hole format
Compact: 4¼" by 6¾", 6-hole format

Here's a summary of available forms.

Project Timetable. Use this form to establish project timelines and priorities and to track costs.

Project Planning Form. Thinking a project through at the beginning is the key to its efficient and organized completion. This form helps you clarify goals, set target dates, identify resources, and establish budgets.

Meeting Planner. This form will help you define the purpose of the meeting, the place it is to be held, the agenda, any preparation that is needed, and who should attend.

Information Record. Record ongoing communication on this form.

Project Task Map. Use this form to map out your project, chart your progress, and diagnose what you need to do next.

For information about the Franklin Covey "Planning for Results: A Practical Approach to Project and Workload Management," call (800) 767-1776.

BEST-BET FILING SYSTEM

YOU WILL NEED:

- File cabinets, cubes, or boxes
- Hanging folders and labels
- File folders and labels
- If you work with an assistant, one stacking letter tray for a "To be filed" basket

SETTING UP NON-PROJECT FILES

A messy desk and office may be the result of an ineffective or nonexistent filing system that doesn't aid in the management of paper flow. Many people fear filing stuff away because they don't trust their ability to retrieve it quickly and efficiently. Any filing system is only effective if it helps you retrieve information.

Many people seem to have a knack for organization and setting up filing systems that work perfectly. The rest of us need a simple system that gives us confidence that we will be able to find something once it's filed away.

This Is Your *Life*

Your filing system should reflect *your* life. It shouldn't follow some artificial guideline out of a textbook. So while it's nice to have listings of typical file headings, it's more important to know what categories make sense for *you*. Just as you break a project down into hunks (major pieces), chunks (minor pieces), and bites (tasks), so will your life-information be broken down into manageable pieces. The perfect tool for beginning this breakdown is mindmapping. In the center of a sheet of paper write "Info" or some symbol to represent the information you want or need to keep. You may want to use sticky notes so you can move and recombine your headings. Your first categories might be "personal" and "work." For this appendix, we will only concentrate on work files, so you would mindmap "Work info," and you might come up with some of the following:

Clients
Contacts
Prospects
Competitor Information
Survey Results
Marketing
Sales
Conferences
Direct Selling
Reports
Training
Product Catalogs
Finance
Budget

Think of these categories as the major pieces of your filing system. The minor pieces are the individual file folders. Some of the major pieces are so big that you will want to devote entire filing drawers to them. Others may be adequately served with a Pendaflex folder made up of two or three files.

Once you have your major pieces, you will continue mindmapping the major pieces into subcategories to develop the labels for individual file folders. For example, "Reports" might break down into Quality Control Reports, Labor Utilization Reports, and Client Status Reports.

It is helpful to use broad, general headings for file categories rather than narrow, specific, hard-to-remember headings. The key to effective retrieval is clear, meaningful identification of file categories and folders. This means clear and meaningful to you and to anyone else who needs to use the filing system.

TIP—The key word should always be the first word of the label. Use specific, unambiguous nouns rather than adjectives, adverbs, dates, or numbers. It is harder to find "1995 Sales Report" than it is to spot "Sales Reports." If dates are important, put them at the end: "Sales Report—1995."

Creating a File Map

Since the most important aspect of a file system is ease of retrieval, it's a good idea to create a file map. This map is the final result of your mindmapping exercise, and it can be posted by your file drawers or in some other easily accessible reference location. The map provides a visual guide to filing new material. Otherwise you might file a catalog under the vendor's name one time and under "Catalogs" the next. If you decide that all vendor catalogs will be filed together, your map will remind you of that decision and help develop file consistency.

TIP—Alphabetical filing is sometimes helpful within a major category. Categories such as "Client File" and "Prospect File" would benefit from an A–Z subcategory breakdown so data can be filed by name. For this reason, loose-leaf notebooks are sometimes better than standard folders for these kinds of files.

SETTING UP PROJECT FILES

Project files differ from other files because a project is temporary. The file you choose to set up will depend on the size and duration of the project. For most small projects, one 8½ x 11" file folder may be adequate to hold all the necessary information. For large projects, a cabinet full of file folders may be necessary. Sometimes you may want to use a large notebook that can hold several inches of paper. A combination of these may be desirable.

Regardless of the type of project file or notebook you use, when a project is active, put a project tab in your day planner to help track the management of project information. This will include any data that can help you manage the project—task lists, Gantt charts, mindmaps, notes, and so on. Several kinds of files may be attached to a project: computer files, file

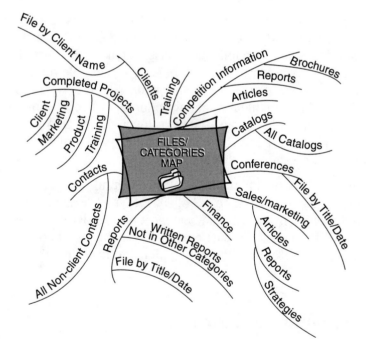

FIGURE B-1
File Map, Mindmap Style

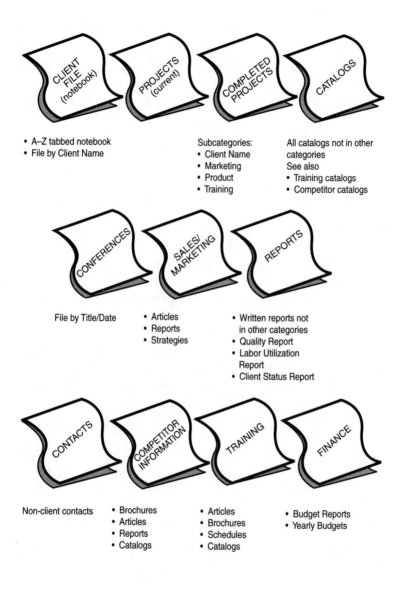

CLIENT FILE (notebook)
- A–Z tabbed notebook
- File by Client Name

PROJECTS (current)

COMPLETED PROJECTS
Subcategories:
- Client Name
- Marketing
- Product
- Training

CATALOGS
All catalogs not in other categories
See also
- Training catalogs
- Competitor catalogs

CONFERENCES
File by Title/Date

SALES/MARKETING
- Articles
- Reports
- Strategies

REPORTS
- Written reports not in other categories
- Quality Report
- Labor Utilization Report
- Client Status Report

CONTACTS
Non-client contacts

COMPETITOR INFORMATION
- Brochures
- Articles
- Reports
- Catalogs

TRAINING
- Articles
- Brochures
- Schedules
- Catalogs

FINANCE
- Budget Reports
- Yearly Budgets

FIGURE B-2
File Map, Post-It Note Style

folders, and notebook files. The key to retrieving information is, first, to clearly identify the name of the file on the file label or tabs, and second, to use parentheses in your day planner to indicate where the information is stored (see Chapter 8). Make "Projects" one of the major categories in your file system, and then establish subcategories for "Completed Projects," "Pending Projects," and "Project Ideas."

GETTING IT FILED

Before you file any document, ask yourself three questions:

1. Do I really need to keep this piece of paper?
2. Is it someone else's job to file this?
3. Can I get a copy of this from someone else if I need it later?

Filing is complicated by trying to keep too much stuff that is not important. Your best friend at this point may be the round file. Trash it if at all possible! I once heard an office consultant say that when she went in to help someone organize an office, she threw away 90 percent of what was there—90 percent!

When you handle a new document that needs to be filed, decide on the category and filename, write it on the top of the document or on a small Post-It note placed on the top of a document, and drop it into a "to be filed" letter tray. These documents should be filed daily if possible, definitely at least once a week. If you do your own filing, keep file folders, labels, and your file map handy so you'll be able to quickly create the new file and put it in the appropriate area.

TIP—An automatic label-maker will help you keep your files clearly identified and professional-looking. By having the label-maker handy, you can avoid procrastination and make reading and identifying file labels easier.

HOME FILING SYSTEM

Creating a home filing system is similar to the process described above. Home filing categories might include:

Finances
Company Benefits
Automobile
Household
Travel
Book Notes
Contacts
Appliances
Electronics
Computer
Medical
College
Legal
Real Estate/Property
Investments

Subcategories (file folders) in the "Automobile" category might include Title and Warranty, Repair Receipts, and Automobile Insurance.

"Finances" might include these subcategories: 401k Plan, Cash Flow Reports, Retirement Plan, and Retirement Articles.

Subcategories under "Travel" might be Delta Frequent Flyer Miles, United Frequent Flyer Miles, Maps, Cruise Information, Cannon Beach, Oregon, and Sedona, Arizona.

BIBLIOGRAPHY

Franklin, Benjamin. *The Autobiography and Other Writings.* New York: Penguin, 1986.

Lehmkuhl, Dorothy, and Dolores Cotter Lamping. *Organizing for the Creative Person.* New York: Crown, 1993.

Schrage, Michael. *No More Teams.* New York: Currency Paperback, 1989.

Smith, Hyrum. *10 Natural Laws of Successful Time and Life Management.* New York: Warner, 1994.

Thompson, Charles "Chic". *What a Great Idea!: The Key Steps Creative People Take.* New York: HarperPerennial, 1992.

Winston, Stephanie. *The Organized Executive.* New York: Warner, 1983.

Winwood, Dick. *Creating Quality Meetings: Latest Techniques for Mastering Group Communication.* Salt Lake City: Franklin International Institute, 1991.

Winwood, Dick. *Time Management.* Salt Lake City: Franklin International Institute, 1990.

Wycoff, Joyce. *Mindmapping: Your Personal Guide to Exploring Creativity and Problem-Solving.* New York: Berkley, 1991.

Wycoff, Joyce, and Tim Richardson. *Transformation Thinking: Tools and Techniques That Open the Door to Powerful New Thinking for Every Member of Your Organization.* New York: Berkley, 1995.

INDEX